Climbing

in
Santa Barbara, Ventura, and San Luis Obispo

Steve Tucker
Kevin Steele

Warning
Don't Trust This Book!

(Disclaimer)

The authors have tried to make the information in this guidebook accurate. However, they realize that it will contain errors. Therefore, use it at your own risk. Realize that you are responsible for your own safety. It would be foolish to trust the information in this book instead of your own judgment.

Any number of problems may exist in the text. Route descriptions may be inaccurate or misleading. Difficulty and protection ratings may be incorrect. Route lines may be drawn incorrectly on photographs. There could be other problems. Sometimes you may simply overestimate your own ability, use gear incorrectly, or fail to adequately maintain your gear or physical condition. It's up to you to recognize your own limitations and to seek out competent instruction if you need it.

There is a safety section in this book that may prove helpful. Simply reading this guide does not constitute adequate preparation to climb safely. Even capable and experienced climbers sometimes make mistakes. This can lead to trouble, and if it does you (or your survivors) must accept responsibility rather than blaming the authors or publisher of this book. If you cannot agree to these conditions, the authors forbid you to use this book as a climbing guide. In fact, they suspect that anyone who would blame a guidebook for personal misfortune is probably mentally unfit to be a climber in the first place.

If you do use this book as a climbing guide, that means you agree to the conditions on this page.

Good luck. And hey. . . have a good time out there.

Climbing
in
Santa Barbara, Ventura, and San Luis Obispo

Printed by
Lorraine Press
Salt Lake City, Utah

Information for future guidebook updates can be sent to:
Steve Tucker and Kevin Steele
P.O. Box 1147
Santa Barbara, CA. 93102

Foreword

Quite a few freeway miles lie between the Santa Barbara coastline and any climbing meccas most of us have heard of. I found this the hard way, while attending college there, having to spend an inordinate number of a weekend's precious hours in the car to get to cliffs with a national reputation. At the time I could reel off the exact fraction of a day it took to reach Yosemite, Joshua Tree, Tahquitz, even the Pinnacles. The Needles had yet to be discovered, at least by anyone I knew.

But now, fifteen years later, it's not those long drives I remember, but the short ones to the hills behind Santa Barbara. Up there is where I could find the kind of experience that made climbing an intimate part of ordinary life. Sure, I'd plan and anticipate long weekends to distant destinations, but equally would I dream of sequences of moves on Gibraltar's T-Crack, or especially, on Cold Springs Dome's Makunaima, which had just been discovered. When I walked around campus with wounds on the backs of my hands, I wasn't advertising notorious cracks in the Valley, but the unsung fissures just behind campus. Maybe I hadn't heard of the local climbing before coming here, but it certainly had plenty to teach me about the sport. And even if Santa Barbara's diminutive cliffs never gain the national recognition accorded their big brothers elsewhere in California, they will never be surpassed in their beauty and accessibility.

Plenty of times I remember being chilled by fog on the coast, wondering whether to cancel the morning's planned outing to the hills. If you are caught in a similar dilemma, don't hesitate to jump in the car: often as not you'll discover the rocks up there perched in blue sky and sunshine, warm and full of play, the clouds like a skirt at their feet. You won't even think of long drives to distant meccas. You'll want nothing more than what you have.

—John Harlin III
Author of *The Climber's Guide to North America*
Editor of *Summit: The Mountain Journal*

Opposite Page:
Libby Whaley on first ascent of The Wind
Beneath Her Wings. *Photo: Steve Tucker.*

"*They say that every man needs protection
and they say that every man must fall
yet I swear I see my reflection
somewhere high above this wall.*"

—Bob Dylan

In memory of John Tucker

Preface

The original guide to Santa Barbara and Ventura has been out of print for several years, so a comprehensive update and revision seems in order. Since before the time of that first guide book, it has been a dream to see the entire tri-county area incorporated under one single book cover. Thanks to Pete Gulyash, author of the San Luis Obispo area guide, that dream is now a reality.

This book would not have been possible without the enormous support and input given by Amos Clifford. Without his writing, design, and computer expertise the final product would definitely have been less than what you now see before you.

The real enjoyment of writing a guide book is in the research. It's been great fun continuing the exploration of the area, and checking out all the new routes and formations people have told us about. We hope you'll take the time to read the geology section. It was put together in hopes of giving a better understanding of the rocks we climb on locally. The research into historical information has been most enlightening. Following ever-branching leads back in time we've searched to see who was climbing what, with whom, when, and how. It hasn't always been easy prying open some of the older brain cells to get a clearer picture of the past.

Trying to establish just who did the first ascent of a particular formation or route was a challenge in itself. One group, or "clique" of climbers, can be completely unaware of the exploits of other groups in the area. Compound this effect over several generations and you get the general idea. There were a lot of rumors to be sorted out. We had to put on our Sherlock Holmes hats more than once to get to the bottom of things.

As is evident from all the new routes, people are still plying the hills for more first ascents. Some of the newer lines are somewhat obscure or contrived; nevertheless, every so often a classic is discovered. This on-going pursuit gives evidence that the sport is alive and well. Hats off to those who continue to explore and establish quality climbs!

We have intentionally excluded climbs located on private property where access is in question. To those who have provided us with such information we wish to extend our thanks, however, we ask that climbers respect the rights of all property owners.

The sport of climbing is made up of many things: from bouldering to big walls, frozen waterfalls to mountaineering, and all the other facets that lie in between or tacked on the fringes. There is the desire to do climbs you've seen, heard or read about, or maybe only dreamed of. There is the endless array of equipment and gadgets, and the many books and magazines on how to, why to, where to, and who did what oh-so-gloriously (or not so gloriously). There are also friendships and bonds made that only a climber can know and understand.

We hope that this book might be a catalyst to help you discover the personal adventure, challenge, joy, and contact with the outdoors that is at the very heart of the sport.

Good climbing!
Steve Tucker and Kevin Steele

Acknowledgements

We would like to extend special thanks to the following people, without whom this book would not have been possible:

Amos Clifford of Technical Assistance Associates, Visalia California, designed and typeset this book and amused us with his reminiscing. **Peter Gulyash** for his invaluable assistance with the San Luis Obispo section.

Yvon Chouinard for his support, historical information and his monumental contributions as a driving force in the local scene and to the sport as a whole.
Lost Arrow Corporation provided production support.

Tanya Atwater, Bruce Luyendyk, and **Helmut Ehrenspeck** for their help with the geology section. **Reese Martin** & **Dana Hollister** for their input regarding the Ojai area.
Dick Blankenbecler for his original Sespe Gorge notes.
Herbert Rickert for taking us back into the earliest days of tri-county rock climbing. **Campbell Grant** for use of his Chumash rock art reproductions. **John Hankins** for allowing us access to the Sierra Club's rusty dusty Condor Calls of yester-year.
John Harlin III and **Gene Miya** for filling us in on history of the UCSB Mountaineering Club.

In addition, the following people have provided valuable help and information: Sue Atwater, Menzo Baird, Tony Becchio, James Blench, Pat Briggs, Kevin Brown, Tim Brown, Steve Edwards,Chuck Fitch, Mike Forkash, Rusty Garing, Jon Goodman, Dave Griffith, Bruce Hendricks, Ken Klis, Tim McMahon, John Merriam, Connie Papsøe, Stuart Ruckman, Ed Sampson, Dick Saum, the GRC, and all those who contributed photos and artwork.

Cover Photograph is of Dave Griffith leading Makunaima.
Photo by Frank Brodarick.
Photo this page by Tim Brown.

Chumash rock art designs based on original art by Campbell Grant.
Illustrations on pages 18, 186 by Dorie Hutchinson.
Illustrations for Foreword and pages 40, 138 by Lori Peterson.
Maps on pages 42, 43, 44, 45 by Sue Atwater.
Condor art on page 19 by Carl Buhl.

All photographs and artwork are by
Steve Tucker and Kevin Steele unless otherwise noted.

Table of Contents

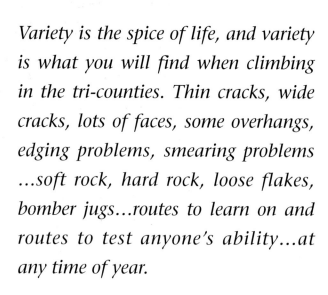

Introduction

Variety is the spice of life, and variety is what you will find when climbing in the tri-counties. Thin cracks, wide cracks, lots of faces, some overhangs, edging problems, smearing problems ...soft rock, hard rock, loose flakes, bomber jugs...routes to learn on and routes to test anyone's ability...at any time of year.

Climbing in the tri-counties is a year round affair. We are blessed with a Mediterranean climate which provides an average annual temperature of 72 degrees with only moderate amounts of rainfall. The south coast and its environs provide the local climber and those passing through with a great variety of short to medium length routes. Most of the climbing here is on sandstone and as is typical with sandstone, the quality can vary greatly. Be aware of the fragility of this medium, particularly after a rainstorm. Not all the rock is sandstone, however. The rock outcrops in San Luis Obispo and southern Ventura are a superb blend of volcanics while an outcropping of compact, edgy Blueschiste can be found at the Kryptor above Santa Barbara. There are even hidden spots of limestone, and in the backcountry of San Luis Obispo you can find conglomerate formations that attempt to mimic those found in the Pinnacles National Monument.

There are dozens of routes within each county. Good routes, bad routes, easy routes, rad routes. While probably half of the routes lie on the larger and more popular formations, the other half are scattered about on small outcrops or hidden in canyons. We have tried to collate all this information into some semblance of logical order. This is not a guidebook for a single crag, there are over 400 routes throughout three big counties. To help you out we have recommended the best routes in each area using the common star system.

If you are a local, we hope this guide will lead you to new explorations and provide you with a much needed reference to our crags.

If you are visiting, passing through, or simply thinking about traveling here someday, we hope that this guide can get you around as well as impart a flavor of what climbing on the south coast is all about.

History

J ust how long ago anyone first stepped onto one of the south coast's rock faces in any way that resembles what we know as technical rock climbing has never been clearly established. From what is known of the Chumash Indians it is obvious that they loved to be among the rocks and did a fair amount of scrambling to access sacred caves and crags. No doubt the earliest Spanish settlers scrambled amongst the rocks in search of riches in the mountains. For our purposes, we need to look a little closer to the present day.

The Early Years Sierra Club records from 1950 describe climbing outings by local members to areas outside of the tri-counties. John Cross was probably the most active of this group. Whether or not he or his contemporaries actually did any local ascents during this period is not known. It is very likely that if climbing was done before the early fifties at the local crags, it was in the form of rappelling and possibly a little top-roping.

The climbers of the fifties and early sixties took with them a rack of pitons and typically a 120 foot length of manila or nylon "goldline" twisted rope. A bowline-on-a-coil took the place of a modern harness and climbing shoes were likely to be tennis shoes, work boots, or the less common European kletterschue.

The first known technical climbing of a south coast crag was done by Herbert Rickert in 1954. When Rickert first saw Gibraltar Rock it was, in his words, "a vertical jungle." The main ledge halfway up the south face was overgrown with thick brush, as were the top edges of the formation. It took a considerable amount of "gardening" to establish a clear path up the route now known as *The Ladder.*

Opposite: Herb Rickert, Rick Knight and John Hestenes on Gibraltar Rock, early 1950's. Photo: Dave Armstrong collection.

*Some of them were dreamers
and some of them were fools
who were making plans
and thinking about the future.
With the energy of the innocent,
they were gathering the tools
they would need
to take them back to nature.*

from *Before the Deluge*
by Jackson Browne

Rickert also did the first known ascent of a difficult crack on Gibraltar's West Face. He used wooden pegs hammered into the crack for direct-aid climbing. The climb quickly gained notoriety and inspired the locals to call it *Herbert's Horror*. The climb later became known as the *T-Crack*. Rickert was accompanied on many of his climbs by his friends Dave Armstrong, Bob Trefzger, and Robert Lockard.

During the early to mid 1950's John Graham, a well-to-do Montecito resident, became known for his mountaineering travels in the Alps, Mexico, and Africa. He often carried with him a heavy Bolex movie camera to record his ascents. Although not active in the local rock climbing scene, it is noteworthy that over a period of 15 years Graham had climbed all the peaks in the U.S. over 14,000 feet. During the summer of 1951 he climbed all 23 of the peaks over 14,000 feet in the Alps and in 1952 he climbed all the peaks over the 14,000 mark in Mexico. By the age of 62 Graham had set a record by having climbed 102 different peaks over 14,000 feet.

By 1956 other climbers had started to occasionally visit Gibraltar Rock. Rickert had fixed *The Ladder* route with pitons so that the rock would not be damaged by repeated placement and removal of pins. In the late 1950's someone contacted the *Santa Barbara News Press* telling them of the climbing activity. The subsequent article in the newspaper brought more climbers to the crag. To the dismay of Rickert and his friends, one of these new arrivals removed the fixed pitons.

It was during the fifties that the Sierra Club's outing section began to use Gibraltar Rock for rock climbing. Herb Rickert was asked to be the first leader of these local trips. Subsequent Sierra Club climbing outings during the 1950's and 1960's were lead by climbers such as John Cross and Bob Trefzger. Mike and Bill Loughlin of the Sespe Chapter also helped with the outings making them some of the earliest known climbers from the Ventura area.

Into the '60s By 1960 Rickert had climbed *The Nose* at Gibraltar using pitons for direct aid. It was also during the late fifties that Rickert first led both the *Cave Route* on Cathedral Peak as well as the *Tree Root* via the start of *The Long Climb* route at Sespe Gorge.

When Yvon Chouinard moved his climbing equipment business to Ventura in the 1960's he brought with him not only his renowned climbing abilities, but he and his business also attracted fellow climbers who were excellent cragsmen in their own right. This list included climbers such as Tom Frost, Tex Bossier, and Dennis Hennek. In 1965 Chouinard and the locals from Stoney Point and Tahquitz made the first recorded ascents at Ventura county's Mugu Rock, a great practice location that was easily accessible. By 1966 they began to explore Ventura County for its climbing potential, and during this period put up many of the first lines around the Sespe Gorge and Ojai area. It goes without saying that, from before the time he moved to Ventura until this day, Yvon Chouinard has been a key driving force on the south coast and for the sport of climbing worldwide. His many high-quality first ascents, technological innovations, as well as political, ethical, and environmental efforts have kept him at the forefront of every facet of the sport.

Yvon Chouinard hand-forging pitons in Ventura as Tom Frost looks on, circa 1960. Photo: courtesy of Yvon Chouinard

During the mid-1960's and early 1970's the popularity of rock-climbing increased markedly. At UCSB a mountaineering club was formed. Members such as Dick Blankenbecler and William Thompson established additional routes at Sespe Gorge.

One Sierra Club member, Margaret Young, was not only a rock climber but an experienced mountaineer as well. She, too, frequented both Gibraltar Rock and Sespe Gorge. A remarkable woman with several degrees from Stanford University, she was also a pilot and a licensed aircraft mechanic. Margaret was by no means the only woman climbing in the area during this period. The Sierra Club outings very often had women participants.

In San Luis Obispo, Bob Garing and his son Rusty Garing, along with Ed Sampson, recorded ascents dating back to the late 1960's. They noted signs that climbers had frequented Bishop's peak even earlier than this, but no record has yet surfaced of who these climbers were, what routes they did, or when they made their ascents.

By the mid to late 1960's these early south coast pioneers had climbed most of the obvious routes at Gibraltar Rock, Sespe Gorge, and Bishops Peak, and had free-climbed some of the older aid routes. These were the days of climbing shoes like RR's (Royal Robbins), with a few individuals still wearing the old Kronhoffer style soft leather European kletterschues. Nylon kernmantle ropes had become the favorite to use (but many people still used the braided goldline ropes developed for sailors). This was also a time when pitons were still the mainstay on the average rack. You can still see the pin scars on many local crack climbs.

The 1970s If there ever was a "Golden Age" of climbing in the tri-counties, it was during the 1970's. More major formations were discovered and explored, more old aid lines climbed free during this period than during any other time period to date. Outdoors shops actually started to sell climbing gear. And for the first time a sense of a climbing "community" emerged.

Up until this point in time, climbers enjoyed—some would say cultivated—a reputation as social outcasts. Climbing was not yet considered a mainstream "sport". This soon changed. The seventies saw the marketing of climbing as an "in" sport by manufacturers and the media. Climbing began to take on new dimensions of acceptability and popularity.

As more people took up climbing, more routes were put up.

There was a steady flow of repeat ascents on established routes. Those that once had many loose holds were now almost devoid of even lichen. The faces of the cliffs themselves were starting to change. Often, a route became easier if it had fewer loose holds or more difficult if missing a key hold. As the fragile character of the rock became increasingly apparent, climbers started to use more chocks and fewer pitons. "Clean" climbing eventually became the norm.

It was in the beginning of the 1970's that the first climbing shops opened up in Santa Barbara and San Luis Obispo. The Mountain Sports store opened around 1970 in San Luis Obispo and Upper Limits opened its doors in Goleta in 1971. Others were soon to follow. Granite Stairway opened outlets in both Santa Barbara and San Luis Obispo during the mid-1970's. Yvon Chouinard's shop in Ventura was constantly growing and was now called the Great Pacific Iron Works.

If there was ever a golden age, it was the 1970's

The early seventies continued to see new routes, both from activists in Ventura and the members of the UCSB Mountaineering Club, as well as the Sierra Club climbers. Tim McMahon took over most of the climbing trips for the Sierra Club during the 1970's and was often accompanied by his good friend Bill Bancroft. It was McMahon that put up the *Bolt Ladder* route near Gibraltar Rock in 1969.

Bancroft has the distinction of being possibly the first person to climb at the now popular Lower San Ysidro Canyon cliff. He did a solo aid climb back in the late 1960's using pitons, although it is not known which line he climbed. McMahon occasionally took groups to the Lower San Ysidro Canyon cliff for top-rope practice in the early seventies.

San Luis Obispo's first recorded ascents on lead were made by people like Ed Sampson, Mike Cirone, Rusty Garing, and Dwight Kroll. They put up routes such as *The Hanging Teeth, P-Crack,* and *Flakes To Fresno.*

By the early to mid seventies most people wore RD's and PA's (named after famous French alpinists René Desmaison and Pierre Allain, respectively) or similar specialized rock climbing shoes. Soon to follow was a new and greatly improved rock shoe called the EB that quickly became the most common rock shoe worn by climbers. The EB (designed by British climber Ellis Brigham) was the forerunner of today's highly technical and diverse selection of rock shoes. Climbing ropes were now typically 150 feet in length. Calcium carbonate—gym chalk— had yet to make its appearance on the climbing scene.

By the mid-seventies the newest generation of local hot-shots were starting to make a good showing in the tri-counties as well as other areas around the country and the world. Steve Gerdson of Santa Barbara (probably one of the first people to free-climb *The Nose* route and *T-Crack* at Gibraltar) was burning up the hardman routes in Yosemite. Soon to become a UCSB professor, Jeff Dozier even had a dome in Tuolumne named after him.

Tobin Sorenson played a major role in the development of the San Luis Obispo area by free-soloing what were probably first ascents on many of the major formations in the county. He was known as being the first person to have climbed such notable routes as *Sgt. Peppers Lonely Hand Jamb,* and *Inner Sanctum.* In his prime, Sorenson rivaled the likes of Henry Barber on the world scene. Although Tobin accomplished much while climbing locally, he didn't keep a record or tell anyone specifically what he had done. Unfortunately, this knowledge went with him when he died from a fall in the Canadian Rockies.

Rick Mosher's opening up of San Ysidro Canyon in Santa Barbara was one of the greatest displays of first ascent activity in the entire area. It was Rick's vision and ability that made San Ysidro one of the finest local climbing crags. Mosher was also instrumental in bringing together the Santa Barbara climbers as never before. He seemed to know just about everyone who climbed in the area and would often have big dinner parties with everyone invited to bring a few photos of their latest adventures. Rick died in the late seventies in an airplane crash while on a search and rescue mission in the Sierra Nevada.

It was also during this time that the first ascents at Cold Springs Dome were made by Amos Clifford, Steve Tucker, Steve and Chuck Fitch, Gary Anderson, and Mike Forkash along with their respective partners.

The late seventies saw a significant change in first ascent activity. Up until this point the vast majority of new routes had ascended the more obvious crack systems. As fewer and fewer cracks were available for first ascents, climbers started looking to the unclimbed faces between the cracks. In order to protect

Steve Tucker leading the first ascent of Magic Bag. *Photo: Chuck Fitch*

leads on these "blank" sections of rock, more and more bolts began to sprout on the cliffs. At areas such as San Ysidro and Foothill Crag people were able to climb just about anywhere. It became a bit of an art deciding which lines were the most deserving of something so permanent as bolt protection. This careful selection of bolted routes has, to this day, helped to preserve most formations from over-bolting.

Chalk was now becoming more widely used. As piton scarring of the rocks had all but ceased, white chalk marks were cropping up everywhere lending a sort of "connect the dots" look and feel to routes. Camming devices were introduced as the newest technological improvement for crack protection. Climbing ropes were now typically 165 feet in length. Climbers were switching from swami belts and homemade harnesses to the forerunners of today's modern, manufactured buckled harnesses.

Doug Hsu and Chuck Fitch were, without a doubt, leading the first ascent scene when it came to bouldering around Santa Barbara. This strong team established Painted Cave as the area's number one bouldering spot. They created a majority of the existing problems including such classic routes as *Static Eliminator, Heavy Traffic,* and *Big Deal.* Hsu and Fitch pushed the free climbing limits of this era on many of the harder roped climbs. They also upped the ante by free-soloing climbs such as *The Nose* and *T-Crack.*

Others such as Pete Gulyash, Ed Sampson, Brian Smith, Jeff Smith, and John Harlin III were all climbing at very high standards. Dana Geary was one of the more active women climbers in the Santa Barbara area during this period. Mike Forkash and Gary Anderson teamed up during this time period on new routes such as those at Gold Chasm, Gibraltar Gully, Cathedral Peak, and in Rattlesnake Canyon.

Pete Gulyash has been a leading activist in the San Luis Obispo area climbing from the seventies through the present. He has been involved in a number of quality first ascents as well as being a master of local boulder problems.

Kevin Brown, Curt Dixon, and Thor Archer were all active in establishing a number of first-rate lines both around Santa Barbara as well as in Ventura county. These routes included classics such as *Vanishing Flakes, Great Race,* and *Lie-back Annie.*

By the late seventies and early eighties Ventura resident Rick

Ridgeway was making a name for himself as a top-notch, world-class alpinist with ascents ranging from South America to the Himalayas.

In 1978 Dwight Kroll and James Blench published *Happy Climbs,* the first climbing guide to the San Luis Obispo area.

Menzo Baird and Kevin Brown are two climbers who have continued to impact the local scene for many years. From the seventies, through the present, they have firmly established themselves as key driving forces behind a number of first ascents in all three counties.

Rusty Garing leading
Thin Man *at*
Bishop's Peak.
Photo: Steve Tucker

The 1980s and into the '90s

Mike Forkash started the decade off by becoming the first to do a free lead of the classic *Makunaima* route at Cold Springs Dome in 1980. Bruce Hendricks, Menzo Baird, and Kevin Brown became very active in the Santa Barbara area, establishing classic routes such as *Fine Line* and *Self-Reflection*.

Steve Tucker published the first guide to Santa Barbara and Ventura in 1981. Subsequent guides to the San Luis Obispo area were written by Peter Gulyash in 1986. Gulyash's book *Completely Off The Wall, A Climber's Guide to Bishop's Peak* is still in print. Ken Klis came out with a revised guide titled *Bishop's Peak and Environs, A Climbers Guide* in 1990. The original guides by Kroll, Blench and Tucker are now out of print.

During the eighties Reese Martin started what was to become virtually a one man show at Foothill Crag and Shelf Ridge just outside Ojai. Martin put in over fifteen new lines, some of which were done free-solo, during a period of less than two years. His route *Chummin' For Splatter* is one of the hardest routes in the Ventura area. In the early nineties Dana Hollister was the driving force for establishing new routes at Matilija Wall, in traditional ground-up style.

Menzo Baird, Pete Gulyash, John Merriam, Hans Florine, Tim Medina, Mike 'Ski, Ed Keefe, and Flint Thorne have led San Luis Obispo from the eighties into the nineties with quality routes like *Camel, Lama,* and *Humps.* Merriam's route *Jet Stream* and Baird's *Meltdown* are the hardest routes to date in the SLO area.

The eighties saw a decrease in the popularity of direct aid ascents. Although often accompanied by aid techniques to place protection, free climbs of much greater difficulty were being sought after far more often than extreme aid routes.

Up until this point, public climbing competitions were unheard of except in Russia and parts of Europe. For many people, the very idea of an organized competition was totally against the grain of the sport. Right or wrong, things changed. Climbing competitions are now regularly held on artificial walls with holds that can be readily rearranged to form different routes and difficulties. In the latter part of the decade this trend was due in great part to the increased popularity of "sport climbing". This newest style of free climbing generally gravitates towards extremely steep, overhanging, difficult, short (one pitch or less) routes, with protection bolts usually closely spaced and often placed on rappel. Artificially constructed climbing walls have for some become popular as a sport that is in many ways distinct from traditional climbing.

Dave Griffith, Pat Briggs, Jon Goodman, Ted Stryker, Tony Becchio, Hans Florine, and Phil Requist have made an impact on the Santa Barbara scene during the late eighties and early nineties by putting up a number of difficult new routes. Most notable of these routes are probably *Pseudomania* at Upper Gibraltar, *Crank Start* just below Gibraltar Rock, *Kneeanderthal* at Cold Springs Dome, *Hazardous Waste* near the Bolt Ladder wall, and the climbs at the Kryptor formation. The most difficult free climbing routes in the Santa Barbara area have fallen to Dave Griffith. *The Quartz Crystal* at the Kryptor is a tribute to his abilities. Griffith as well as Jonny Woodward have also pushed the bouldering limits at Painted Cave with routes like *Trojan* and the *Hallway Roof.* Pat Briggs has become the most prolific first ascensionist in our local history. His exploration and inspiration have been behind many of the more recent routes in the Santa Barbara area.

The newest style of "free climbing" gravitates towards extremely steep, overhanging, difficult...

Jade Chun has put the women climbers of the area on the map by climbing at an extremely high level of difficulty worldwide. Libby Whaley is another local woman who has contributed several first ascents in the Santa Barbara area. Other women such as Rosie Andrews, Maria Cranor, Schatzi Vandehei and Molly Gibb have also helped to firmly establish a place for women on the crags.

During the later part of the eighties the ever growing litigious nature of our society started to take its toll. The first outward signs of this appeared in 1988. The Sierra Club's insurance carrier announced that they needed $500,000 more per year in liability premiums to cover any climbing outings. The club decided to drop their climbing and mountaineering activities rather than incur the extra cost. The UCSB Mountaineering Club was also done away with by the legal overseers of the University System for fear of liability. The business end of climbing was about to be tethered by outside forces. In the years that followed, the traditional freedom of the climber would be the next victim of restrictions brought on by the courts, insurance companies, lawsuit-crazy "victims," fear of legal repercussions, and last (but not least) irresponsible actions by climbers themselves.

As the nineties rolled around, the spectre of lawsuits and the "deep pockets" mentality figured greatly in Yvon Chouinard's decision to divorce himself from his climbing equipment business. This was, no doubt, an emotional as well as a difficult decision for a person and company whose foundations were so deeply rooted in the sport of climbing. It has yet to be determined just how much further this form of legal arm-twisting will affect a sport that has prided itself on its non-conformist, individualistic, and adventurous nature.

On a positive note, UCSB Adventure Programs and Cal Poly's ASI Outings Club have, for several years, provided climbing classes to both students and the general public. This is especially good in light of the community's loss of the Sierra Club's climbing section.

Toward the Future

The mountains above San Luis Obispo, Santa Barbara, and Ventura offer many more route possibilities for future generations. The big problem in discovering and developing new areas has been, and will be, accessibility.

Climbers can help shape the future of the sport by being increasingly aware of, and active in, community decision-making processes regarding preservation and development of open areas. By setting examples through responsible actions at the crags we can help ensure continued access to areas now available to us, and at the same time take steps towards opening up those areas presently restricted from public use.

Opposite: Crank Start—
Dave Griffith on his
Gibraltar testpiece. Photo:
Pat Briggs

"Climbers will not just be getting from bottom to top, but will in effect be writing a score"

—*Royal Robbins*
in Advanced Rockcraft

Route Descriptions

Just as artists give titles to works of art, or skiers name downhill runs, climbers love to name their routes. Route names can run the gamut from serious to humorous, historical to whimsical, often outrageous and completely unrelated to the nature of the climb itself. Sometimes a route name comes from a song, book, or movie. Sometimes a name may come from something so unrelated to climbing that only the person who thought it up will ever understand it.

At Cold Springs Dome, for some obscure reason, the first routes were established with names from the *Felix The Cat* cartoon. It was hoped that eventually any and all routes put up at the Dome would be similarly named. Although a number of the route names have followed suite, there are also routes whose names are derived from other origins.

The difficulty rating of a climb is usually established by the first ascent party and is indicative of not only the style in which they climbed, but also of the condition of the rock at the time. Respecting the first ascent style of a climb preserves the original nature of the rock and the route for future generations. Placing additional fixed protection on a route lowers the quality, adventure, and difficulty of the climb.

A first ascent means different things to different people. For those on the original climb there is the pride of creating and the thrill of adventure that anybody gets from doing and seeing something for the very first time. There is also the knowledge that you have made a contribution to the sport both physically as well as historically.

It has always been a source of great interest as to who climbed what, when, and how. Not only is the historical perspective interesting, but it acts as a sounding board for future climbing parties. First ascent information gives us something by which to gauge our own abilities, style, and even our ethics.

Route Description Key

FA	First ascent (first lead of climb).
FFA	First free ascent on lead.
TR	Route normally climbed with a top-rope, rather than on lead.
FTR	First top-rope of climb.
X	Bolt.
P	Fixed piton.
(R)	Runout (protection is sparse with the chance of a long serious fall).

Terms and Definitions

Free climbing is getting up the cliff without hanging or resting on your equipment. You are propelling yourself up the rock using your hands and feet with ropes and gear used as a safety in the event you fall.

Free-solo (or "Third Classing") is when someone climbs alone without the backup or aid of ropes and hardware.

Aid climbing is when a climber is resting, hanging, swinging, stepping, pulling, or otherwise dependent upon equipment to get up or stay on the rock.

Solo climbing simply means you are climbing by yourself and this can be with or without the use of ropes, etc..

Bouldering generally refers to climbing without the use of ropes and hardware on rocks to a height no greater than about fifteen feet (often less).

Top-Roping means that the belay rope and its anchor are above you while climbing.

Star Ratings

We've incorporated a *star rating system* to help identify those climbs of note in the area. This system reflects the quality rather than the difficulty of a particular route:

★ Enjoyable, recommended.

★★ Worth repeating, high quality.

★★★ An excellent route, the best the area has to offer.

"In wildness is the preservation of the world"

—Henry David Thoreau

Preservation

Climbing areas are frequented by people other than just climbers. We as climbers must respect the fact that others have as much right as we do to enjoy the wilderness in its natural state. We must also realize that many of the approaches to the crags are via easements or adjacent to private lands, and that our access privileges could very easily be taken away if abused. With an ever-increasing climbing population, the need to take care of our natural resources has become more critical than ever. With this in mind, we must do whatever it takes to ensure the continued access and use of the mountains and crags. This starts with a few basics.

Although it is rarely the climbers who leave trash lying about, carrying out a little trash each time you visit the crags will go a long way to clean up the mess left by the less thoughtful.

We may not be able to prevent all the graffiti defacing the rocks, but we can help clean it up and speak out against it. Chipping or gluing additional holds falls into the same category. If you want to alter something, do it back in suburbia or at the artificial wall.

To the non-climber, white marks and bolts all over the cliffs are offending and unnatural. If you use chalk or place fixed pro keep it to a minimum.

There are no latrines at any of the mentioned climbing sites. If nature calls, bury feces well away from drainages, trails, and climbing areas. Also make an effort to carry out the TP.

The local hills are very susceptible to forest fires year-round. Campfires are illegal except at approved sites. For some reason, some smokers think it acceptable to toss their spent cigarettes anywhere they choose. Besides being a potential fire hazard, cigarette butts along with discarded bottles and cans are some of the most common litter items found in the mountains.

Don't disturb or harm wild plants and animals. In many areas of the local mountains some falcons, hawks, and condors are endangered species. Some plants are also endangered. The effects of civilization take their toll. Whether it be more houses dotting the mountain sides, motorcycles roaring along trails, or litter from hikers and shooters, we lose a little more of the natural wilderness habitat every year.

Climbers may easily recognize the aesthetic beauty of natural lines of ascent that exist on rock faces. Sometimes we forget to see what is so obvious to non-climbers: the appeal of the untouched rock itself. With this in mind, we would like to make a request of those who are active in establishing new routes in the area. There are certain places where people go to enjoy the mountains in their untouched, natural state. In these places permanent hardware such as bolts or pitons are very much out of place. Indian rock art sites, Lizard's Mouth, The Playground, and any of the waterfall faces are just a few of the locations that fit this description. No matter how tempting the climbing may be, we must respect those who would simply sit and trace the fall of the stream or the weathered face of a boulder without wishing to see a trace of iron, chalk, or sling.

It is very easy for us to disregard those things that make the mountains so attractive. We should recognize how fragile the wilderness is and how hard, if not impossible, it may be to regain if lost. The effects of irresponsible actions harm not only the wilderness, but destroy what we seek in the wilderness for ourselves.

Forecast: Another Gorgeous Day

—Santa Barbara News-Press

Weather

With relatively mild weather throughout the year there is no single climbing season. There will, however, be short periods during each of the four seasons when it will be unpleasant to be out on the crags.

During the spring, usually around June, there is a cool foggy season. The fog is often restricted to a "marine layer" below about the two thousand foot level. There are times when it might be cool at the lower elevations, but hot and sunny at formations such as Gibraltar Rock, Cold Springs Dome, Sespe Gorge, and the Summit Blocks at Bishop's Peak. This fog layer can be welcome on the hotter days as well as being an obstacle if you don't know where the rocks are located.

The months of July through October are the hottest times of the year with temperatures at times exceeding 90 degrees.

In the fall there is an "Indian Summer" from September through early November. This is a condition where the warmer desert air from the east is drawn over the mountains and out to sea ("Santa Ana winds"). Indian summer weather is hot and dry with temperatures at night often reaching as high as 75 degrees or more. The fall can also bring short periods of rain.

November through April is generally the coolest as well as the wettest time of the year. Arctic storm fronts blow out of the Gulf of Alaska and can bring with them an occasional frost, rain, and every so often a light dusting of snow on the tops of the local peaks.

Aside from a few short periods of unsettled weather, the climate on the south coast is usually very agreeable for climbers year-round.

Camping

T he following are a few of the available campsites in the tri-counties. Camp only in marked, designated campgrounds!

San Luis Obispo *El Chorro County Park*: Highway 1, five miles west of the intersection with Highway 101. Close to Bishop's Peak.

Montaña De Oro State Park: On the beach, not close to the crags.

There are a number of remote campgrounds located in the national forest north and northeast of San Luis Obispo.

Santa Barbara *Gaviota, Refugio, and El Capitan State Park*s are all located off Highway 101 along the coast north of Santa Barbara.

There are several campgrounds over the mountains north of Santa Barbara at Lake Cachuma or along Paradise Road off Highway 154. The Paradise Road sites are near to Gold Chasm.

Ventura *Camp Comfort County Park:* Creek Road off Highway 33 just south of Ojai.

Dennison County park: Off Highway 150 just west of Ojai.

Several campgrounds lie along Highway 33 north of Ojai. *Wheeler Gorge Campground* is probably the best of these sites.

Lake Casitas Recreation Area: Off Highway 150 east of Ojai. Located at Lake Casitas.

McGrath State Beach: A more improved site on the beach just south of Ventura's harbor and the Channel Islands National Park headquarters and visitor center.

Point Mugu State Park: Along the coast just off Highway 1 south of Oxnard and Port Hueneme. Usually crowded.

Faint to my ears came the gathered rumor of all lands: the springing and the dying, the song and the weeping, and the slow everlasting groan of overburdened stone.

—J. R. R. Tolkien

Geology

A climbing guide would not be complete without a discussion of the nature of the rocks themselves. The geologic makeup of the tri-counties is diverse, complex, and as interesting to study as it is to climb. Combining the knowledge of several sources we have attempted to put the information in as non-technical terms as possible.

The easiest way to view the majority of the area's geology is to picture it much like a layer cake. Over many millions of years, layer upon layer of different sediments were deposited in varying thicknesses. Some formed on ancient ocean floors while others built up in river flood plains or vast, shallow inland water basins. These sediments were buried by succeeding layers, compressed with tremendous pressures at great depths and cemented together by dissolved minerals transported in ground water. They formed the sandstones and other sedimentary rock types we see today. The layers have since been uplifted into mountain ranges. In some spots magma has pushed up into and through the layers to form volcanic crags. Over time, erosion has worn away the softest layers to expose the harder rock faces. It is on these more durable outcrops that climbers have found the area's best routes.

Natural History In order to better understand the rocks and mountains of the tri-counties, we need to first travel back in time almost 250 million years. New sections of the earth's crust, called "plates," were being formed by magma welling up through weaknesses in the mid-Pacific sea floor. This constant generation of new seafloor material spread the already formed ocean floor farther and farther apart. The "sea-floor spreading" was slowly pushing parts of the ocean crust towards North America.

During the Mesozoic Era (the age of dinosaurs), the Farallon Plate was approaching the west coast. The Farallon, along with other portions of the sea floor, did not just slam into the conti-

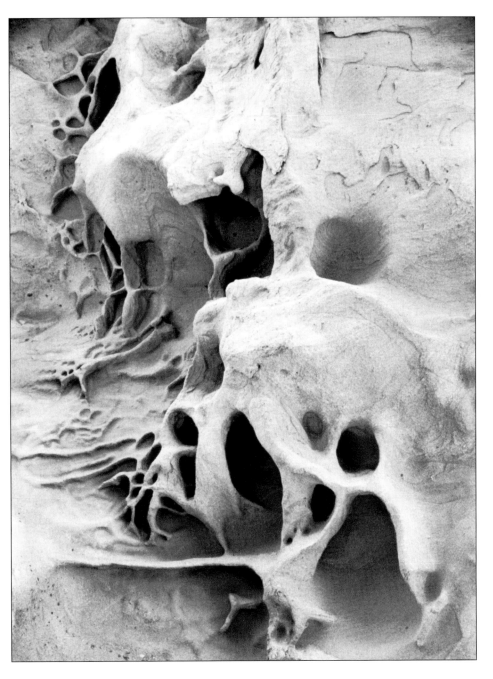

Chemical weathering.
Photo: Steve Tucker

nent. In a process called *subduction,* the sea floor was constantly diving under the coastline. This caused some very interesting things to happen. The continent's coastal edge, riding over the subducting plates, acted much like a bulldozer by scraping off the topmost layers of the ocean floor. This plowed-up debris, plastered on the coastal edge, is the jumbled array of rocktypes known as the Franciscan Formation (containing the Kryptor crag). As the ocean plates dove deep under the continental edge and down into the earth's hot mantle, parts of the plate material melted back into magma. Some of the magma leaked back up to the surface, forming a line of volcanoes (similar to the Cascades). Other magma didn't make it to the surface and eventually cooled at depth. It hardened to form the granite *batholiths* that make up the core of the Sierra Nevada range.

40 years ago climbers appeared in the local mountains, depositing pitons, slings, bolts, and chalky sediments.

During the Paleocene Epoch, 65 million years ago, the tri-county area was part of the shallow underwater continental shelf extending east to the base of the ancient Sierras. This time period was also when mammals first started to appear on the earth. Sand, silt, and clay washing down out of the Ancestral Sierras were deposited on the shallow sea floor. These were the sediments that would make up the Juncal formation. Hermit Rock, on East Camino Cielo, is a good example of the sandstone portion of this structure. The Juncal was the first and deepest of the area's sandstones to be deposited. These initial layers not only have had longer time to be more strongly cemented together, they have also been subjected to the greatest compression of all the local sedimentary strata, making them the hardest.

About 10 million years later, during the Early Eocene Epoch, sediments from the same source started to create the Matilija Sandstone. The Matilija forms crags like Gibraltar Rock, Cold Springs Dome, Sespe Gorge, and the Matilija Wall. The Coldwater Sandstone of Lower San Ysidro Canyon, Cathedral Peak, Foothill Crag, and Lower Mission Canyon was deposited another 10 million years later and hence subjected to less compression and cementing action than the Matilija, making for a somewhat softer rock in the end.

Around 25 million years ago, the East Pacific Rise (the center of the seafloor spreading) entered the subduction zone. It was at this point that the Pacific Plate first made contact with the North American continent. As the younger, hot, buoyant seafloor material of the East Pacific Rise was subducted, it uplifted the overriding continent. This was the period during which the landmass that would later become the tri-counties first rose above sea level. Some of the sediments washing down out of newly created mountains built up on flood plains, eventually becoming the cobble and pebble-filled conglomerates common to the local Sespe formation and probably the massive outcrops of Castle Crags.

During the next several million years the contact of the Pacific Plate with the North American Plate created the San Andreas Fault and a number of subsidiary faults and weaknesses. It was along one such weakness that magma flowed up, spewing forth onto the surface and giving rise to the Morros of San Luis Obispo.

The continued northward movement of the Pacific Plate along the San Andreas Fault was by no means a smooth process. Large chunks of the continent's edge were ripped off and dragged along. Baja California was one such chunk that was pushed up into Southern California. Another piece, making up much of the tri-county area, broke free and was slowly rotated between the Pacific and Continental plates. This massive action twisted our local mountains into their unusual east-west alignment. Continued movement along the San Andreas Fault system then gave rise to the Santa Ynez mountains. The once horizontal, neatly stacked layers of sediments were now being tilted and pushed into the uneven shapes of today's peaks and valleys.

The youngest of our local sandstones is the Vaqueros Sandstone. These sediments were deposited about 24 million years ago in a low basin that had probably been pulled open within the complex San Andreas system. This is the same rock that is found at Point Mugu. It was also during this same time period that local oil deposits began to accumulate.

Beginning about 3 million years ago a series of events started to sculpt the local mountains into the features we now see around us. First, the mountains were gradually thrust several thousand feet higher than they stand today. At the same time intense erosion, brought on by a period of unstable weather during the ice age, washed large amounts of soil and rock from the mountain slopes. As the softest soil and rock weathered and washed away, the toughest layers were left protruding as the best climbing surfaces. Even today the local mountains continue to be slowly uplifted, and at the same time worn away by erosion.

Man first migrated to the area about 12,000 years ago, but didn't settle in any sort of permanent fashion until around 8,000 years ago (enter the Chumash Indians). Juan Cabrillo, a Portuguese explorer sailing under the flag of Spain, landed along the Santa Barbara coastline in 1542 becoming the first European known to have set foot in the tri-counties.

About 40 years ago climbers, as we now know them, appeared in the local mountains depositing pitons, slings, bolts, and lately white chalky sediments.

Rock Types

Sandstone

Sandstone is derived from the buildup and layering of eroded grains of rock sediment over long periods of time. Great pressures were placed on the sediments as they were buried deeper and deeper. This pressed the grains tightly together. The closely packed grains were then glued (or cemented) together by minerals in ground water such as silica, iron, and calcium carbonate from dissolved shell material. Quartz, dissolving readily under pressure, can also re-deposit to create a very firm bond. Matilija Sandstone contains a great deal of quartz.

The individual shape of the grains themselves plays a big part in how well the rock is bonded. Angular grains tend to interlock and hold much more strongly than rounded grains and are more readily bridged by any cementing agents.

If clay particles are abundant in the cement, moisture can cause the clay to expand and soften, thus separating and weakening the grain bond.

Although the Matilija Sandstone is a denser material than other local sandstones, it is also more brittle. With tectonic and seismic movement within the earth continuing to disturb the formations, an enormous amount of microscopic fracturing (even within the grain structure) can create a very absorbent rock. Water, allowed to get into the structure through these minute

Hands jammed into a crack, feet
dancing on concoidal fracture planes.
Tony Becchio leads T-Crack *on Gibraltar Rock.*
Photo: Pat Briggs.

cracks, can then dissolve the cementing agents and weaken the stone. This can happen even if clay particles are not present in the matrix.

Until the cements can dry out and re-bond the grains, the rock may continue to be weakened. This is an important thing to know if climbing after a rain.

Pockets and Ripples

Common to sandstones are depressions, bulges, ripples, small pockets and shallow caves. Large, wave-like patterns such as those seen on the west face of Gibraltar Rock are concoidal fracture planes (like you sometimes see in chipped glass) where a large chunk has broken away from the main rock. These patterns are usually associated with thick bedded or massive, uniform sandstone. However, the ripple patterns seen at the Bolt Ladder are fossil evidence of water action when the sediments were first laid down.

Smaller pockets and dished-out areas can be created by an *inclusion* (a pebble or rock within the sandstone itself) weathering out, leaving a void. This inclusion could also have been a soft clay or shale lens (blob) that has dissolved away.

Chemical weathering can also create holes or even caves. Where cracks are often associated with a weakness in rock, hairline cracks can be a channel for transporting dissolved, durable, cementing minerals. The dissolved minerals can re-deposit in and around the cracks, thereby making the crack's structure very erosion resistant. Natural salts and lime, along with water, working as corrosive agents, can then dissolve the surrounding, softer rock, leaving the mineral-strengthened crack structures protruding as raised ridges. It is not unusual to see this type of formation under an overhang (where moisture tends to concentrate) making up what looks like a ghostly web of pockets and interconnecting ribs. The roof under Lizard's Mouth, the large pockets at the Fire Crags, as well as the seam/ridge that makes up the Hazardous Waste route are (although strikingly different) examples of this type of action.

Chemical weathering can also work in the opposite way. Very fine fractures in the sandstone (often where hairline cracks intersect) create a centralized weak spot. The natural corrosive agents, mixed in water, can dissolve the crack structure as well as the surrounding rock itself.

Rarely does wind alone play the major role in creating any of the features discussed here. It is the combined work of the corrosive minerals and water that, more often than not, is the cause of crumbly, rotten surfaces on the sandstone.

Cracks

Cracks in sandstone are also formed in several ways. The first is from faulting. This is when major sections of strata shift along one plane causing a split between them.

Interbeddings are thinner layers of softer rock separating the main sandstone layers of the formation. Very thin to chimney sized cracks can result when these interbeddings are eroded away.

Cracks can also form when invisible or hairline seams are widened by water. Water generally acts on the rocks in several ways. One method is where water, carrying sediments, flows over the rock surface. Acting like liquid sandpaper, it erodes troughs or grooves. This action is often in conjunction with an already present weakness or depression in the rock.

If water seeps into cracks and freezes, it expands and pushes on the sides of the crack, thereby widening it. Water seeping into thin seams can also react with corrosive minerals within the stone and cause a seam to widen by chemical erosion.

Plants, particularly bushes and trees, are extremely effective in opening up cracks by the force of their burrowing and expanding roots. This is more common with already partially detached blocks, slabs, and flakes.

Edges and Knobs

Sandstone may have a harder surface layer. This is caused by minerals within the formation being wicked or transported to the surface by moisture. Often a mixture of iron, magnesium, manganese oxides and hydroxides form a very hard, dark plating called a *varnish* or *patina*. Drying and oxidation at the surface hardens these minerals into a shallow crust.

This varnish can take tens of thousands of years to form. Color and thickness of the varnish can indicate how long the surface layer has been exposed and be an indicator of a rocks stability. As portions of the surrounding surface areas erode away, the climber is left with knobs, plates, and flakes of the harder mineralized layer to climb on. The south face of Gibraltar Rock is a good place to see evidence of this.

Color

The color of sandstone is dictated by the minerals present in both the cements and the sand grains themselves. Color can also be a tell-tale sign of how hard or soft the rock surface might be. Red, rust, brown, tan, yellow, black and ochre usually indicate iron or manganese in various states of oxidation (an excellent example of this coloration can be found at the Brick Yard). White powdery areas are often lime deposits. Generally speaking, the darker the surface of the sandstone, discounting lichen and moss, the harder it is.

Long vertical weeps or drip stains on a face can occur from either minerals within the stone leaching out or from soils or other rock types being washed down the cliff face by rains.

Volcanics

There are outcrops present both in southern Ventura county as well as in the hills surrounding San Luis Obispo formed by volcanic processes.

Ventura's Santa Monica Mountains are actually upwellings of magma through fissures in the older, surrounding sedimentary formations. The magma formed intrusive plugs, dikes, and pods below the surface. Violent eruptions also spewed lava out onto the surface to form thick layers of jagged debris. The rock itself is know as *dacite breccias* and *andesite*. Erosion eventually exposed the outcrops we see today.

The hillsides or *morros* strung between San Luis Obispo and Morro Bay are actually volcanic plugs. They are the result of a common fault or fissure through which magma could rise. The lava erupted out onto the surface to build up volcanoes. The last of the lava within each volcano didn't quite make it to the surface. This material cooled and hardened in the throat of the volcano. Erosion has since worn away the surrounding hillside to expose the core or *plug* within the volcanic cone. The remaining rock is known as *dacite,* a hard, fine grained rock flecked with larger crystals called *phenocrysts.*

Grain size within volcanic and igneous rocks is often a telltale sign of both how fast the rock cooled as well as how close to the surface it solidified. Typically, rougher surface texture (larger crystal grains) indicates that the rock cooled more slowly and deeply underground.

The holes and pockets found in the rocks are air bubbles that came out of the lava by outgassing (much like bubbles come

Holes and pockets typical of volcanic rock of San Luis Obispo. Photo: Steve Tucker

out of champagne). This happened as the lava reached lower external pressures near the surface of the earth.

Cracks can be formed as the lava cools and shrinks. Cracks can also be formed by faulting during seismic activity. Some fractures and pockets have been widened by erosion. Others have been acted upon by concentrated corrosive gases and chemicals from within the rock itself.

Metamorphics

The Kryptor climbing crag, just over the main Santa Ynez ridge to the north of Montecito, is probably the most unusual rock we have. As part of the Franciscan Assemblage it is one of the oldest rock formations in the area.

Made up primarily of Blueschist, Kryptor was created by great pressure and at great depth. The outcrop is actually a large, disconnected block that has been brought back up to the surface from almost twenty miles deep. In the process it has mixed in with the surrounding shattered jumble of rock types known as the Franciscan Assemblage. The quartz from which the route Quartz Crystal derives its name was formed after the initial uplifting.

The extent of irregular fracturing in the rock is from the process of being dragged and tumbled up to the surface from such great depths.

There are a number of sizeable boulders in the area of Nineteen Oaks, just up the trail from the Gold Chasm climbing area. These outcroppings are red chert; a beautiful, dense rock with some very interesting features. The hike itself is worth the effort just for the scenery.

Conglomerates

Castle Crags in the Machesna Wilderness of San Luis Obispo are the most striking conglomerate cliffs in the area. They are composed of pebble and cobble inclusions surrounded by a hardened clay matrix. The cobbles, along with clay sediments, were deposited on an ancient river flood plain. Much of the formation has eroded away, leaving the isolated outcrops protruding from the surrounding mountainside. The distinct red color of the outcrops is from oxidized iron.

Limestone

Although there are limestone outcrops scattered throughout the area, most are either poorly accessible or on private land. The more obvious of these crags are in the vicinity of Highway 166 east of Santa Maria. Others can be seen as narrow whitish bands of rock stretched across the slopes of the San Rafael Mountains behind Santa Barbara.

It is interesting to note that prior to the construction of Bradbury Dam at Cachuma Lake there was a 200 foot high limestone cliff known as Bee Rock between Hilton and Tequepis canyons. The area is now privately owned. But what is worse (from a climber's point of view) is that much of the crag was quarried in 1952 for construction of the dam (and continues to be quarried today).

". . . one more bolt would make it accessible to many more climbers. One more bolt would also rob it of a tremendous amount of its atmosphere, excitement and challenge, of its spirit and so of its quality. It would become just another route. . . "

". . . it is much better to improve our abilities, whatever that may entail, than to lower the climb. "

—Peter Gulyash
A Climber's Guide to Bishop Peak

Ethics

Given enough time, individual climbing areas tend to establish their own set of standards. The tone that is set is usually influenced by a number of things; the nature of the rock itself, technology, climate, but ultimately it is the climbers themselves who set the standards.

Traditionally, climbing has been a very individualistic activity and what anybody does, more or less, has been thought of as their own business. This gets a bit messy as the number of climbers increases and the number of readily available first ascent possibilities decreases.

The challenge in climbing is to try and overcome the problems presented by nature with the fewest crutches. Man has always used his ablility to make and use tools to assist him in his endeavors. Climbing is no exception. The more we use technology, the easier the challenge is to overcome.

The sport of climbing has always had, and no doubt always will have, on-going debates as to what constitutes right and wrong. It seems to be the nature of the animal. One thing is certain, the natural resource that we climb on is a finite resource. There are times when what seems like the new direction for the sport to take, turns out to be a fluke. History tells us that for every new innovation or radical new approach, there is almost inevitably an uproar or debate about its appropriateness. History, however, will also show us just which of these approaches has been lasting in its effect on the sport and is looked upon by future generations with any sort of respect and acceptance.

There is an irony in climbing as tool-wielding man attempts to challenge nature on as even terms as possible. The closer the experience is to a one-on-one with the basics, the better. There is an unspoken line over which one cannot step without sacrificing the heart and soul of what we are doing.

A climbing "route" consists of two basic elements; a series of existing features on the rock that lends itself to climbing and the ability of a climber to recognize that potential then actualize it. If the features do not exist or a climber can't visualize any potential, then a route won't be established.

One of the true "artistic" aspects of the sport is when a climber is faced with choosing the cleanest, most aesthetic line for a new route to take up a cliff. This is especially true when a number of potential route possibilities are grouped closely together. Rather than cramming several routes into a small space, the choicest of the lot is chosen leaving the other surrounding possibilities as either not worth the effort or as variations on the original theme. Approaching a climb in this manner lends credence to what has been deemed a "quality line. "

The more you use the natural features of a cliff, the greater the challenge. The less fixed protection, the greater or bolder the challenge. Protection placed on lead makes for a bolder and more challenging ascent, especially for future parties. Less fixed protection leaves the crag closer to its original condition.

By striving to climb "clean" with equipment that does not damage the natural features; by placing bolts only sparingly and on lines well deserving of such permanence we keep the challenge and the aesthetics at a high level. Fixed pitons are even more rare and can be left in place so as to keep from repeated scarring. It is important that techniques and equipment be used that lend themselves to protecting the rock and the environment from our passage for future climbers. Leave the rocks as natural and uncluttered as possible. If you cannot put up a new route in good style then don't hack your way up it. Come back another day when you're more able or leave the route for a more qualified climber to do.

The use of chalk has become so prevalent, that people habitually dip into their chalk bags even on the very easiest of climbs. Often, key holds on routes get so caked with the white stuff that the rough sandstone holds become squeaky smooth. This, of course, leads people to use even more chalk.

Climbers weaned solely on bolted routes will likely find themselves in dire straits if attempting an ascent requiring fundamental techniques in the use of protection equipment and natural protection. Relatively inexperienced climbers can gain a false sense of expertise and security if they have only climbed on routes with closely spaced bolts. If you relegate yourself to climbs requiring only the clipping of bolts you will not only be dependent upon old protection placed by someone else, but you will also be missing out on many of the finest and most creative climbs available.

The out-of-doors has always been the realm of the climber. Even if you are into artificial/indoor climbs, the roots of the sport are grounded in the natural stone of the mountains. What nature and the out-of-doors offers the climber is unattainable anywhere else. The advertising hype and indoor rock gyms can only pretend to offer the real thing. It is when people start to confuse the two that we are in trouble.

There is a reason that so many books and top climbers talk of climbing as an "art" or "craft." Climbing routes with harder moves than previous generations have accomplished does not necessarily make us better climbers. There's a lot more to climbing than difficulty ratings. Think of the less advanced equipment and the greater unknowns faced by earlier pioneers. Style, commitment, boldness, and finesse have always counted for more than the mark of any hammer, bolt, or high-tech gadget. If it were the general consensus that it was acceptable to drill, bolt, sling, glue, or chip anything and in any manner, then climbing would lose something which people have always sought and admired.

How we choose to use or abuse our technological abilities in concert with our desire to push mental and physical limits sets our standards. It has been suggested that "without limits, there is no game."

"It's no game. "

—*Herb Laeger*
(watching a climber
ground-out after an
80 foot leader fall.)

Jade Chun taking leave
of Quartz Crystal.
Photo: Tim Brown

With the best equipment in the world, the man with poor judgement is in mortal danger...

—Royal Robbins
Advanced Rockcraft

Safety

R ock climbing can be a very safe sport; however, the potential for serious injury or death is very real. Most problems arise, as with any other activity, when people don't adhere to the basic rules. Aside from human error, there will always be the ever present objective dangers that are inherent with any climbing experience. Falling rocks, loose handholds, or any of the myriad of other natural hazards should never be taken for granted.

There are more than enough scary stories of mistakes and near misses at the local rocks: there's the fellow showing his buddies how to climb, but his tie-in consisted of a single non-locking carabiner clipped to one of his leg loops. There's the inexperienced guy having the novice girl rappel off the cliff with the ropes only laid over a small rounded knob for an anchor with no top-rope or prussik as backup. There's the stud showing his girl friend how to tie into her harness with completely bogus knots. There's the father taking his family climbing, and belaying the whole group off of one manky quarter-inch bolt. While trying to catch a top-rope fall a belayer lost grip on the belay plate letting the rope uncontrollably feed out with the climber tumbling 40 feet down the face. And how about the guy who topped out on his lead, thought he'd clipped the one anchor bolt...well, when his second slipped and fell, our leader-turned-belayer suddenly realized he'd missed the clip on that ol' bolt, got yanked right off the top of the wall, and the two of them ended up in the gully below. A mom and dad came to the crag with their baby carefully tucked in a bassinet, then set the tyke right down at the foot of the climbs in direct line of rockfall and tossed ropes, etc. (they were politely asked to set the kid well out of harms way). Then there's the "instructor" having his gaggle of students tie their swami belt web-

bing with square knots, and as if to ice the cake...top-roping every- one off a single bolt. And on, and on, ad nauseam. Luckily, none of these mishaps resulted in anyone's getting seriously hurt.

The sobering thing about all of this is that every one of us is subject to the potential consequences of objective and subjec- tive dangers. No matter how good you think you are, or how safe a situation seems. . . double, triple check everything, and back it up. Never take the proper use of technique, judgment, and equipment for granted. If you don't know. . . find out. Climbers have been known to have fairly substantial egos. Arrogance, ignorance, or being overly casual have a funny way of sneaking up and taking people off guard at the most inop- portune times. This can be disastrous when climbing.

If you are a beginner or not well-versed in the particular type of ascent you are about to undertake, make sure you get compe- tent instruction prior to climbing. Understand that there is much to know in order to climb safely—besides clipping bolts—in order to cope with the many varied situations that can arise in the great outdoors.

Before you go blasting off onto the crags, take a little time to understand the particular characteristics of the local hills. If you're used to climbing on granite, you might want to know about the weaker nature of sandstone, especially in regards to placing protection.

If you see someone screwing-up, tell them. There's nothing wrong with reminding someone not to step on a rope or saying that you think they might not have tied-in properly. When you're on top of a cliff be aware of loose rocks that could be knocked down on people below.

About fixed protection Since much of the climbing in the tri-counties relies on the use of bolts for anchors, a few words of caution are in order. Never assume that, just because a route has fixed protection, you don't have to bring along your own pro. Never blindly assume that every bolt, piton, or any other piece of fixed protection is sound.

A word to the wise, just in case you didn't know, don't pound on bolts! If you hammer on a bolt in an attempt to either test or set it better, you'll only weaken it. Several older bolts have been found with serious weaknesses from this form of abuse. Also, several bolts have been placed (most of the known ones have been removed) that are of improper design for placement in sandstone. The most commonly used bolts are 3/8 or 1/2 inch diameter expansion design. Like anything else in climbing, if you don't know what you're doing, don't do it! Place protection deeper in sandstone cracks, especially camming devices. The lips of sandstone cracks have been known to break under the load of a fall.

Another note concerning safety is that sandstone is weakened when it is wet (see the geology section). It is wise to assume that holds and protection on a given route will be substantially weaker after a rain. Be aware of the weather conditions, and go properly prepared.

Arrogance and ignorance have a funny way of sneaking up...

Know how to recognize poison oak. It changes color during the year, and in the wintertime completely looses its leaves but not it's ability to give you trouble.

Rattlesnakes live in the local hills and like to hang out among the rocks. Bats are also common residents in the cracks of local crags, and are known to carry rabies. Ticks may carry Lyme Disease.

A sense of community has grown among the locals. The area's climbers generally know each other, and are accordingly friendly and courteous at the crags. Just because you might be (or think you might be) a better climber than the next, doesn't give you any more rights. So if you're from out of town and someone walks up and points out that your harness looks like it's not buckled right or that you might consider belaying off the two brand-new $1/2$ inch bolts rather than that single 20 year old quarter-incher...try being thankful for their concern rather than letting your ego get the better of you.

Be aware that conditions on the crags change through the passage of time, and that this book only reflects approximate conditions. Fixed and natural protection can weaken, rock features weather, and rights of access change.

There are local all-volunteer rescue teams capable of technical evacuations. In Santa Barbara, the Search and Rescue Group operates under the auspices of the Santa Barbara County Sheriffs Office. **In an emergency, call 911.**

Climbing is a great sport to be involved in, but remember that it is an activity that, without clear and honest assessment of one's own abilities and the conditions at hand, can lead to grave consequences. Understand, also, that being able to do difficult moves and climbing safely are two very separate issues.

Poison Oak
(Toxicodendron
diversilobum)

The authors and publisher of this guide book strongly recommend that you help fight closures and oppressive regulations of climbing areas by becoming a member of the Access Fund by making a tax-deductible donation.

the ACCESS FUND

PO Box 17010
Boulder, CO 80308

Ranchers in the the San Luis Obispo area have closed off fantastic sections of potential climbing. The locals living around Painted Cave in Santa Barbara, seeing chalk marks, have gotten upset about what they thought was graffiti. The original Hot Springs Canyon trailhead above Montecito was closed after the property owners fought a legal battle to keep hikers (and climbers) from passing over a section of trail that had been used by the public for years. Property owner's have attempted to keep climbers and hikers from using public access roads to National Forest land in the Ventura backcountry. The Lizard's Mouth area was once a pristine get-away from the signs of civilization, but it now sports everything from "splat (paint) gun" marks, fire pits, broken glass, beer cans, discarded clothing, etc., etc.

The Access Fund, a national, non-profit climbers organization, is working to keep you climbing. The Access Fund works to preserve access and protect the environment by buying land, funding climbing support facilities, financing scientific studies, helping develop land management policy, publishing educational materials, and providing resources to local climbers' coalitions. Every climber can help preserve access!

Join us in helping to protect our climbing resources, preserve climbers' access, and to promote environmentally sound climbing practices.

Maps

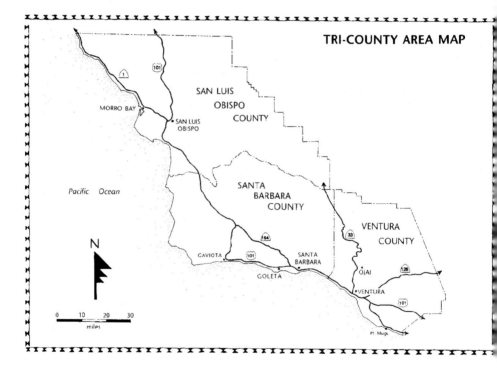

TRI-COUNTY AREA MAP

"Around the corner there may wait
a secret road or a hidden gate;
and though I oft have passed them by
the time will come at last when I
shall take the hidden path. . ."

—JRR Tolkein

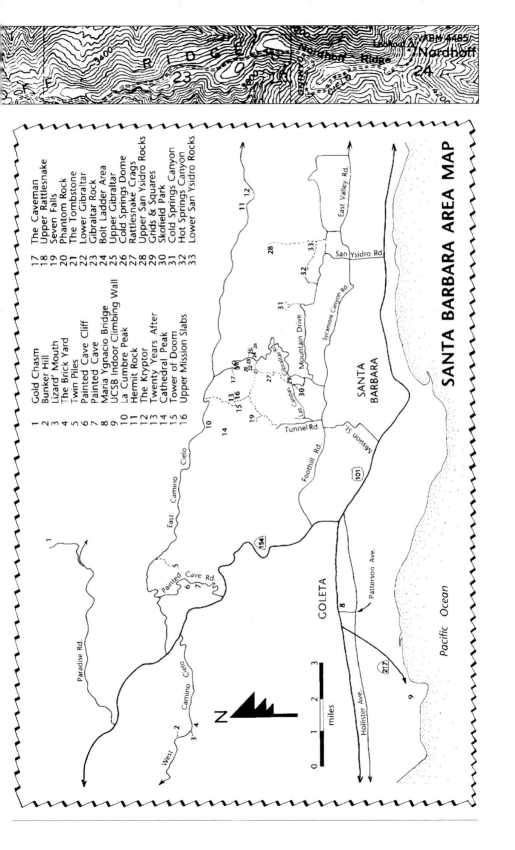

SANTA BARBARA AREA MAP

1 Gold Chasm
2 Bunker Hill
3 Lizard' Mouth
4 The Brick Yard
5 Twin Piles
6 Painted Cave Cliff
7 Painted Cave
8 Maria Ygnacio Bridge
9 UCSB Indoor Climbing Wall
10 La Cumbre Peak
11 Hermit Rock
12 The Kryptor
13 Twenty Years After
14 Cathedral Peak
15 Tower of Doom
16 Upper Mission Slabs

17 The Caveman
18 Upper Rattlesnake
19 Seven Falls
20 Phantom Rock
21 The Tombstone
22 Lower Gibraltar
23 Gibraltar Rock
24 Bolt Ladder Area
25 Upper Gibraltar
26 Cold Springs Dome
27 Rattlesnake Crags
28 Upper San Ysidro Rocks
29 Grids & Squares
30 Skofield Park
31 Cold Springs Canyon
32 Hot Springs Canyon
33 Lower San Ysidro Rocks

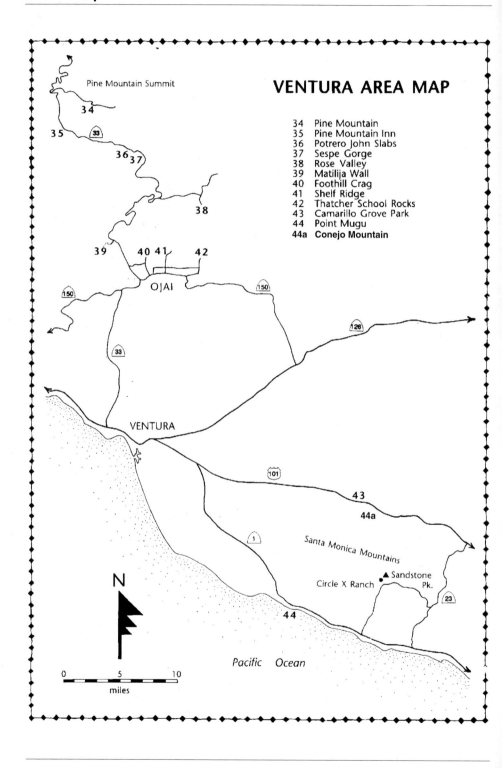

VENTURA AREA MAP

34 Pine Mountain
35 Pine Mountain Inn
36 Potrero John Slabs
37 Sespe Gorge
38 Rose Valley
39 Matilija Wall
40 Foothill Crag
41 Shelf Ridge
42 Thatcher School Rocks
43 Camarillo Grove Park
44 Point Mugu
44a Conejo Mountain

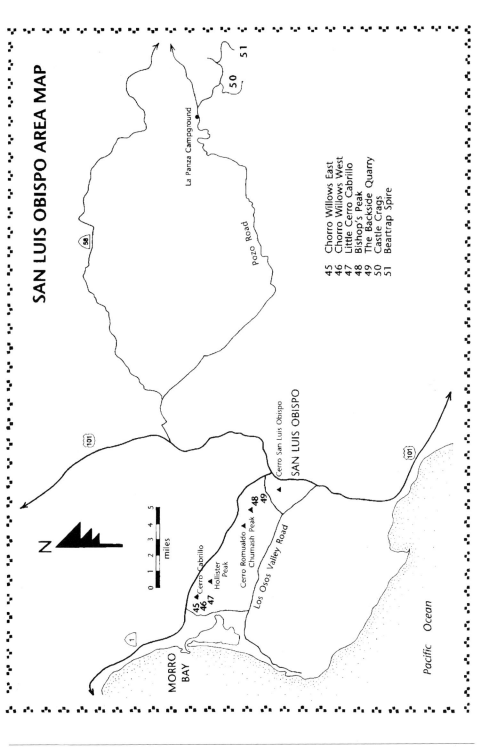

SAN LUIS OBISPO AREA MAP

45 Chorro Willows East
46 Chorro Willows West
47 Little Cerro Cabrillo
48 Bishop's Peak
49 The Backside Quarry
50 Castle Crags
51 Beartrap Spire

Santa Barbara

The rock outcrops of Santa Barbara are not only central in a geographical sense, they also form the original core of climbing in the tri-counties. It is at Gibraltar Rock that the south coast's first technical climbs were done. It is from Santa Barbara that climbers first struck out and explored the potential of Ventura and San Luis Obispo Counties.

San Ysidro Canyon

S **an Ysidro** is one of the more beautiful canyons on the south slope of the mountains and contains two rock faces, the lower of which sees the most climbing.

A year-round creek flows down the canyon, and in its upper reaches forms several pools and small waterfalls. With the climbing areas facing east, the canyon provides welcome shade on hot afternoons. The environment around the creek seems to be the perfect habitat for not only sycamore and bay trees, but to an abundance of poison oak as well.

Take the San Ysidro exit off of Highway 101 and head (north) towards the mountains. Turn right onto East Valley Road then left up Park Lane to Mountain Drive. Turn left onto Mountain Drive. Approximately a quarter mile down Mountain Drive you'll see the trail head on your right (across from the stables). The trail parallels a paved (private) driveway before turning into a dirt road. After ten or fifteen minutes of walking, the lower formation will be seen across the creek on your left. A trail cuts down and left from a wide area in the dirt road and leads across the creek to the rock.

Do not drive or park on the paved and dirt access road that leads up into the canyon at the end of Park Lane West. The trail and access road are easements granted the National Forest by the land owner. It would be a shame if access to the canyon were ever denied because of disgruntled property owners (as has happened in Hot Springs Canyon).

Over the years many top-notch climbers have visited Yvon Chouinard. It was during one of these visits that the famous British alpinist Chris Bonnington was taken by Chouinard to San Ysidro Canyon for a climbing outing. The two ended up doing the first recorded ascent of the Applied Magnetics *route.*

Because of the nature of the rock, San Ysidro is an area where bolts are common. You will also want to take along a selection of nuts to protect some of the routes.

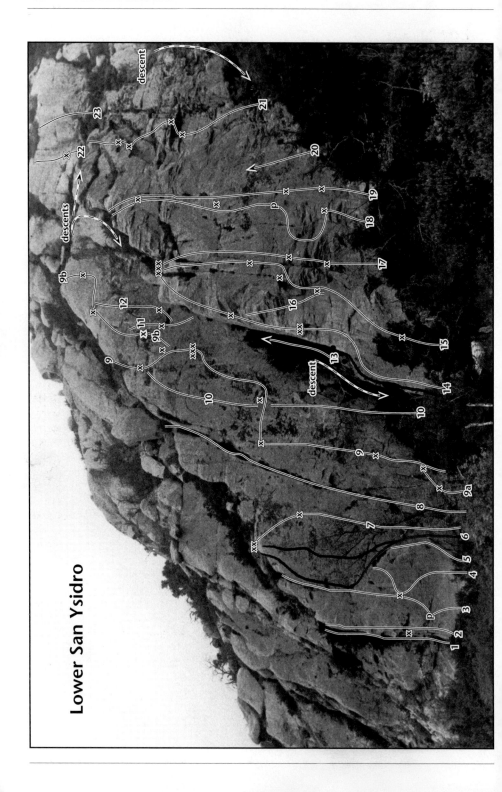

Lower San Ysidro

Lower San Ysidro Canyon

1
Brown Nose Frog
5.8

Ascend the small inside corner and seam at the left-most edge of the main formation and surmount the roof at its top. Wander to the top. Named for the small frog that frequents the route. An oak tree has partially grown over the start of the route. FA Bruce Hendricks, Amos Clifford, and Steve Tucker, March 1981.

2
Puny Prow
5.10

(aka: Over The Edge) Ascend the furthest left outside corner on the formation. A bolt protects the upper moves. FA Bruce Hendricks, May 1983.

3
Vanishing Flakes
★ ★ ★ 5.11a

Lies on the left-hand side of the formation. Climb to the fixed pin under a small roof. Traverse right, then up past a bolt. Follow a seam to easier moves above. FA Tor Archer, Mike Wells, and Howard Eaton, 1976.

4
Young William
5.12a (R)

Climb the face between *Vanishing Flakes* and *Enigmatic Voyage*. Clip the first bolt on *Vanishing Flakes*, then climb face moves up and right of the crack/seam on the *Vanishing Flakes* route. This route tends to be a bit run-out, especially at the beginning (although stacked nuts have been used in a small finger pocket). FA Ted Stryker and John Ford, April 19, 1987.

5
Enigmatic Voyage
5.11b

Ascend the left side of the small arete between *Vanishing Flakes* and *Rockocco*. A boulder problem. FA Soloed by Chuck Fitch, pre-1979.

6
Rockocco
5.5

Just to the left of the large sycamore tree, a right facing corner, with cracks and pockets, leads up and left to a sloping ledge. From the ledge, either climb to the top via a crack (5.4) or up and right (5.7) past a bolt. FA Original Route: unknown.

6a: Right-hand variation (aka: Brush Up): FA Tom Adams and Regan Saunders, October 1978.

7
Applied Magnetics
★ 5.9

Five feet to the right of the beginning of *Rockocco* a thin crack with finger pockets heads directly up the face. Protection is poor just beyond the point where the initial crack thins to a seam (it is possible to incorporate the top bolt on the right-hand variation of *Rockocco*).
FA Yvon Chouinard and Chris Bonnington, mid-1970's.

8
Too Mucking Futch
5.8

Ascends the most obvious crack between *Rockocco* and *Face Lift*. Climb past a small tree and shrubs to the top. Usually a bit dirty. FA unknown.

9
Face Lift
★ ★ ★ 5.7 (R)

This route (and its variations) is definitely one of Santa Barbara's more popular climbs. It was also the first of a series of routes to be established by Rick Mosher in San Ysidro Canyon.

Approximately 20 feet to the left of the gully that splits the main rock faces, climb a flake with its top broken off by either the obvious crack or the easier right side, to a bolt. Head straight up to a third bolt near the *Too Mucking Futch* crack. Traverse horizontally to the right to a fourth bolt (not to be confused with the second bolt on the *Tigger Treat* route). From the fourth bolt head up and right (it gets a bit run-out here) diagonaling to a hole and three belay bolts. Belay and climb up and left past bolts to easy ledges.
FA Rick Mosher and Joe Roland, 1975.

9a. 5.10 (R) Just left of the start, climb the face protected by a bolt. FA Mike Forkash, late 1970's

9b. 5.9 ★★★ From the triple belay bolts, head up (past a bolt) and right into a hole, above which lies another bolt and a few tricky moves. Easier climbing leads up a ramp to the right to a bolt. A few stretchy moves directly right gets you to a ledge. One last bolt protects the final face moves to the top.
FA Rick Mosher and Curt Dixon, mid-1970's.

10
Tigger Treat
5.8 (R)

Follow the crack and seam just right and uphill from the start of the *Face Lift* route. Climb directly to the fourth bolt on the *Face Lift* route. From this bolt head up and left past a second bolt (not on the *Face Lift* route). Join the upper section of the 5.6 variation of *Face Lift*. This route is fairly run-out.
FA Ted Stryker and Zolton Von Somogyi, March 1985.

11
Scrub Job
5.9

Starting about halfway up the left side of the central gully, climb up into the large hole which lies about twenty feet right of the three belay bolts on *Face Lift*. From the hole step out to the left then directly up (5.9) past a bolt to easier ledges above. This is an alternate way to connect up with the upper section of the 5.9 variation of Face Lift.
FA Terry Roland and Steve Tucker, October 1990.

12
Chavez/Mosher
5.10 (R)

Use the same beginning as *Scrub Job*. A bolt above the right-hand side of the large hole protects moves directly up a dished trough. The difficulties don't ease off until well past the bolt. This route was originally climbed as a variation to the *Face Lift* route.
FA John Chavez and Rick Mosher, late 1970's.

Rick Mosher on the first ascent of Face Lift.
Photo: Joe Roland

Seven-year-old Taylor Benson bouldering the start of Enigmatic Voyage.
Photo: Steve Tucker

13
Great Race
★ ★ ★ **5.10a**

This route ascends the steep face on the right side of the gully between *Face Lift* and *Peels of Laughter*. Starting from a ledge with small trees, face climb past five bolts to the top of the buttress. The original route traversed right after the fourth bolt and ascended the arete. The fifth bolt was subsequently added in 1990 to protect the upper face, keeping the route independent from *Peels of Laughter*. FA Curt Dixon and Rick Mosher, 1978.

13a. 5.10b Direct Start: Climb straight up and over the first bolt rather than moving left as is usually done. FA unknown.

Phil Plumb leading Great Race. Photo: Pat Briggs

14
Peels of Laughter
★★5.5 (R)

This line proceeds up the small buttress to the right of the central brush filled gully. The climb is fixed with two bolts later added by Rick Mosher. FA Chuck Fitch (solo), 1975.

15
Many Happy Returns
★★★5.9

To the right of *Peels of Laughter* climb the smooth slab past a bolt. Head up and right past another bolt protecting steep face moves leading to a left facing layback corner. From atop the layback, follow an obvious crack protected by two (somewhat unnecessary) bolts to easier climbing. An excellent and diverse route. FA Rick Mosher and Curt Dixon, 1978.

16
Amish In Space
5.10a (R)

Climb to the ledge below the second bolt on *Many Happy Returns*. Climb directly up past the bolt on thin edges, staying between the easier holds on *Peels of Laughter* and the lie-back flake on *Many Happy Returns*. This leads to a series of bulges. Ascend the bulges directly to easier climbing near the top of the buttress. This is a serious lead, since the only piece of fixed protection is the one bolt. FA John Patterson, December 1987.

17
Orangahang
★★★5.7

Approximately 30 feet up and right from the start of *Many Happy Returns,* climb the steep slot and crack, protected with a bolt on the left side. Climb over a bulge and head for a second bolt. Continue up a crack to the top of the same buttress that contains the *Many Happy Returns* and *Great Race* routes. This route can also be protected without using the bolts.
FA Rick Mosher and Curt Dixon, 1979.

18
Rick's Route
★★★5.7

About 15 feet to the right of *Orangahang,* a bolt protects moves directly left past a bulge with an undercling. Above the bulge move back right and up a trough past a fixed pin and bolts to the top. FA Rick Mosher and Curt Dixon, 1979.

19
Fine Line
★★5.9

Ten to twelve feet right of the start to *Rick's Route,* head for a hole. Up and left of this hole is a dished area with a bolt. Clip the bolt and head directly up the obvious crack and seam past another bolt to easier climbing (a bolt on *Rick's Route* can be clipped off to the left in this area). Climb directly up and slightly right along the obvious seam to steeper climbing past a final bolt.
FA Bruce Hendricks and Toby Cotter, June 1983.

20
Ricky Don't Lose
That Number
5.9 (R)

Unprotected, this route ascends the face between *Fine Line* and *The Weeny Roofs*. FA Chuck Fitch, 1979.

The climb was put up, third class (free solo), on sight, in memory of Rick Mosher.

21
The Weeny Roofs
5.9

Up the hill to the right from the last two mentioned routes, two ceilings can be seen on the face. Starting from below the first roof, climb over the widest part of that roof, past bolts, to a ledge. Climb up and left over a second roof past two bolts to the top. FA Curt Dixon, Rick Mosher, and Mike Forkash, 1979.

The following routes are on the tier just above the lower main wall and right of the central gully.

22
The Heckling
5.10 (R)

This route lies almost directly above the top of the central gully. Friction climb up the middle of the dished face past a bolt (which replaces a bush that was pulled out by a leader fall). The crack on the right is sometimes used to protect the upper moves, but otherwise, the route gets run-out straight up from the bolt.
FA Bruce Hendricks, Steve Tucker, Amos Clifford, March 1982.

23
Teacher's Aid
5.8 or A3

Forty feet right of *The Heckling*, this route originally nailed (aid) the thin seam just right of a right leaning corner. Take small pro. The route was subsequently climbed free by the first ascent team. FA Bruce Hendricks and Mike Milway, March 1982.

There are a number of fun boulder problems to do on the rock-strewn ridge directly above the main formation.

Upper San Ysidro Canyon

Approximately one and a half miles further up the canyon from the Lower San Ysidro formation lies a second group of rock ribs angling down the mountainside. The rocks are on the left (west) side of the canyon and are not visible from the Lower San Ysidro crag.

At a point just before the fire road turns left and crosses the creek, continue on the trail that leads up the right-hand side of the canyon. Follow this trail until you've gone past some switchbacks and a pipe handrail. You've gone too far if you cross a tributary creek entering from the right. The large, slanting formation is seen across the canyon to the west.

Upper San Ysidro

Menzo Baird leading Dinky Pinkys. Photo: Breaton Kelly

The rock ribs on the same slope, both upstream and down-stream, contain more climbing possibilities. There are also a few bouldering spots along the trail to the upper formation.

24
Flaking Away
5.9

Two rock ribs below *Gnome Fingers*. Climb through tree branches past a roof to a crack protected by a fixed pin.
FA Tor Archer and Fiona Wilson, January 1988.

25
Gnome Fingers
★ ★ ★ **5.10**

At the low, left-hand base of the formation, a thin crack comes out onto the face from under a small roof. Follow this crack to easier climbing and the ridge above.
FA Amos Clifford and Joe Roland, mid-1970's.

26
Dinky Pinkys
5.10d

Uphill and to the right of the beginning of *Gnome Fingers*, face moves lead up and left to the point where the thin crack comes out from under the small roof. Follow the rest of the *Gnome Fingers* route. FA Curt Dixon and Jeff Schloss, 1979.

27
No Hanger
5.10

From the beginning of *Dinky Pinkys* climb up and slightly right past a hangerless bolt to the top (hint: take a hanger with you). FA unknown.

28
African Queen
5.8 (R)

Climb the thin crack up-hill from *No Hanger* to a fixed pin, then follow natural weaknesses to the top. There are several long runouts.
FA Bruce Hendricks and Jeff Webb, February 1982.

29
Clifford/Roland
5.7

About 40 feet uphill to the right of *Dinky Pinkys* climb directly through a square notch low on the wall. From the notch, climb straight up via cracks and edges to the ridge above.
FA Amos Clifford and Joe Roland, mid-1970's.

30
Center Path
Boulder

Lies next to the trail in the upper canyon near the large water hole and before the cement paved switchbacks. Contains several fun bouldering routes in the 5.9 range. FA probably by Tor Archer, Michael Wells, and Howard Eaton, 1975.

Dick Saum climbing The Rock on the Coast. *Photo: Steve Tucker*

Hot Springs Canyon

The old Hot Springs trailhead at the upper end of Hot Springs road is now closed due to property owners denying access. To reach the climbs, you must now approach via the McMenemy Trail in San Ysidro Canyon.

31
The Rock on the Coast
★ ★ **5.10**

Hike west along the hillside until you reach the original ridge trail east of Hot Springs Canyon. A group of rocks lies at this trail junction. The second rock mass on the right is a small wall that angles down the hillside to the east. Just off the trail, the overhanging section of this rock, facing the ocean, contains the route *The Rock on the Coast* (5.10). The area around this short jam-crack contains other possibilities.

FA Chuck Fitch and Steve Tucker, April 1980.

Cold Springs Canyon

The Cold Springs Canyon trailhead can be found by driving up Cold Springs Road from Sycamore Canyon Road in Montecito. When you reach Mountain Drive, turn right and continue a short distance to the paved creek crossing. Park and head up the trail along the right side of the creek.

Cold Springs Canyon has a west and an east fork. The west fork eventually winds up at the hairpin turn partway up Gibraltar Road. The east fork of the creek heads up the mountain slopes to Montecito Peak and East Camino Cielo.

Technically the Cold Springs Dome formation belongs under this section, however, the Dome has its own chapter heading and its' approach is from the Gibraltar Rock area.

There are several outcrops of Coldwater Sandstone not too far up the canyon from the the Mountain Drive trailhead. The cliffs are fairly broken and often rotten. There have been, however, rumors of some climbing activity in the area.

Tangerine Falls

Total approach time is about 45 minutes. From Mountain Drive, follow the Cold Springs Trail up the canyon. After walking several minutes, the West Fork Trail splits off to the left at a point where the trail dips near the creek. The trail crosses the creek and heads up the left side of the canyon.

You'll know if you're on the right track if you start to see sections of pipe along the side of the path. About fifteen minutes from the road (3/4 of a mile) the 200 foot high waterfall face can be seen up a side canyon to the right (north). A side trail forks off to the right, down and across the creek bed. Follow this trail up the side canyon (sometimes scrambling or in the creek) to the base of the waterfall. The slabs to the right of the falls afford a good view of the routes.

Opposite:
Tony Becchio leading
Infectious Groove.
Photo: Tim Brown

Tangerine Falls

Photo: Pat Briggs

To reach the base of the climbs scramble up the gully and ledges just left of the waterfall's base. To set up a top-rope belay for the left-most routes continue scrambling up and left to the top of the gully. Head up and to the right until a 20 foot rappel from a tree can be made to the bolt anchors.

32
Fool's Gold
5.10d

Climb the left-most, smooth face that runs the full height of the cliff. Starting just left of the main buttress, climb past two bolts to the horizontal crack. From atop the block/pedestal clip a bolt and follow face moves up and left to the double bolt anchor. FTR Pat Briggs et. al., 1992.
FA Kevin Steele and Kevin Brown, October 1992.

32a. 5.10+ TR. After clipping the first bolts above the horizontal crack, head up and right past a bolt to a double bolt anchor. FA Jake Morgan and Pat Briggs, 1992.

33
Infectious Groove
5.12

Start at a yucca plant on top of a ledge just below the wide crack. Climb up and out the diagonal crack leading out the roof past several bolts. Getting to and over the roof is the crux. Bolt-protected face moves lead to the double bolt anchor above.
FA Pat Briggs and Tony Becchio, October 1992.

34
Cosmic Tarantula
★ 5.10d

From the approach gully, head up slabs to the right. Climb the right-leaning crack in the corner and move left to surmount the roof. Thin face moves (protected by a bolt) lead over the roof. Three more bolts protect the face to the double bolts up above. FA Pat Briggs and Tony Becchio, 1992.

35
Chunky
5.10a

Starting at the base of the slab just right of *Cosmic Tarantula*, climb that slab to the point where it meets the slanting crack. A bolt protects moves over the roof onto the blocks and horns. Climb straight for the *Cosmic Tarantula* top anchor.
FA Jim Tobish, Tony Becchio, and Pat Briggs,1992.

36
Ballistic Midget
5.10b

About twenty feet right of *Chunky*, bolts protect roof moves leading directly to a double bolt anchor on top. A crack on the lower section of the route comes in handy.
FA Tony Becchio and Marty Snyder, 1992.

Gibraltar Rock

Gibraltar Rock is undoubtedly the most popular climbing crag in the area. This can be attributed to its' being right next to the road with easy access to a number of enjoyable routes on rock of excellent quality.

Gibraltar is the first crag in the tri-counties known to have been scaled by roped climbers. From the earliest days to the present, the formation has been used by beginners, climbing classes, search and rescue team practice, and experts alike. It is also a popular hangout for people who like to break beer bottles, spraypaint the rocks, and leave trash strewn about. Here, more so than anywhere, is where climbers must take extra care of the finite resource of rock and wilderness.

To reach the rock, take the Mission Street exit from Highway 101. Head up Mission towards the mountains as far as you can. Hang a left at Laguna Street then a right onto Los Olivos Street. You'll drive right past the Old Mission itself. Keep to the left at the first fork. After a few hundred yards a brown and yellow wooden sign will point you up Mountain Drive. Keep left at the first sharp hairpin turn. Wind up Mountain Drive to the green building at Sheffield Reservoir. Turn left, (still on Mountain Drive) and then right onto Gibraltar Road. Five miles up Gibraltar Road the formation is easily spotted as the large, block-like mass of sandstone west (left) of the pavement.

The parking areas around Gibraltar are also the jumping off points for approaches to Hole-in-the-Rock boulder, the Bolt Ladder, Upper Gibraltar, bouldering in the gully above Gibraltar Rock, Lower Gibraltar, and Cold Springs Dome.

*A*round 1902 work was begun on *La Cumbre Trail* which followed the same path as today's Gibraltar Road. The trail builders named different spots along the way, particularly those points having spectacular vistas or prominent natural features. When they reached the 2,900 foot level on the mountain slope, a large blocky outcrop struck them as deserving of a name. They dubbed it *"Centinela del Abismo"* or *"The Sentinel of The Abyss."* The name soon fell by the wayside in favor of the more generic *"Gibraltar Rock."*

Herb Rickert, Gibraltar Rock, circa 1955. Photo: Dave Armstrong

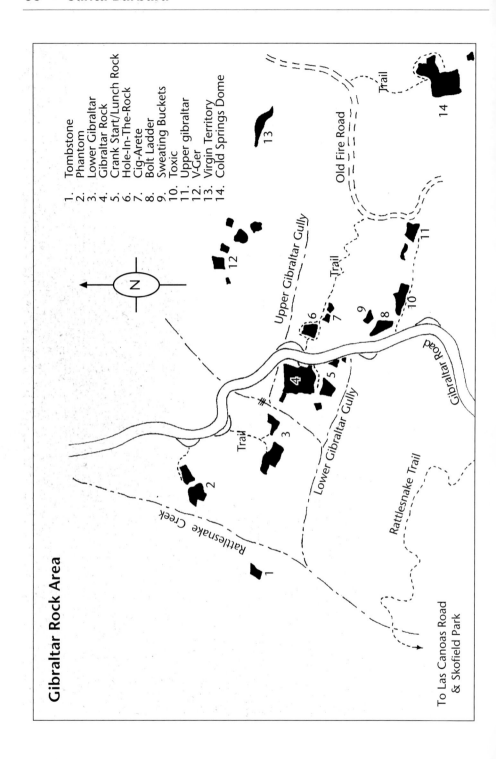

Gibraltar Rock Area

1. Tombstone
2. Phantom
3. Lower Gibraltar
4. Gibraltar Rock
5. Crank Start/Lunch Rock
6. Hole-In-The-Rock
7. Cig-Arete
8. Bolt Ladder
9. Sweating Buckets
10. Toxic
11. Upper gibraltar
12. V-Ger
13. Virgin Territory
14. Cold Springs Dome

N

Rattlesnake Creek

Trail

Upper Gibraltar Gully

Trail

Lower Gibraltar Gully

Old Fire Road

Trail

Gibraltar Road

Rattlesnake Trail

To Las Canoas Road
& Skofield Park

Yvon Chouinard
climbing
Gibraltar's south face.
Photo: Steve Khan

West Face, Gibraltar Rock

Main (South) Face, Gibraltar Rock

Approach Routes on the 70 to 140 foot west face of the main rock may be started from the base of the cliff or from Peanut Gallery Ledge. Most of the lines can be top-roped.

To reach the bottom of the west face, walk and scramble down the trail and gully along the base of the south face.

Peanut Gallery Ledge is reached by way of the gully at the top northwest edge of the rock.

On the south face (facing the ocean) possibilities for variations seem to be limitless. Four routes have been noted that provide the most natural lines combined with decent protection.

If you can, carry out a little trash as you leave.

37
Northwest Corner
5.1

Starting at the tree at the base of the northwest corner, climb that corner to *Peanut Gallery Ledge*. FA Unknown, early 1950's.

38
T-Crack Corner
5.6

This is the small roof and 1-1/4" crack in the corner leading to the main dihedral below *T-Crack*. This short undercling/lieback variation starts in the alcove next to the tree near the base of the dihedral. FA Kevin Brown and Jeff Smith, 1976.

39
Peanut Crack
5.5

Climb the obvious short crack directly above *Peanut Gallery Ledge*. FA unknown.

40
T-Crack
★ ★ ★ 5.10

(aka Herbert's Horror) Either down-climb from the *Peanut Gallery* or climb up any of the routes below it, to the short ledge halfway up the left-hand side of the west face. Climb the only crack leading directly up to the alcove in the middle of the west face. Instead of climbing right into the alcove, traverse out to the left. By way of a poorly protected mantel shelf (5.8), climb directly up to and follow the small ceiling and crack that leads up and right. After about 12 feet, reach up and left to a finger crack and the top. FA Herbert Rickert (via direct aid), 1956. FFA unknown (possibly Jim Donini), pre-1970.

40a. From *Peanut Gallery Ledge,* and just left of the mantel, bypass the mantel move by way of a right leaning flake (5.10). FA unknown.

40b. ★ Just after traversing left from the alcove, climb small face holds (5.10+) up and slightly right off the mantel shelf (unprotected/top rope). FA unknown.

40c. At the top of the standard route, instead of reaching for the finger crack, continue further to the right and reach up (5.10) and into a left-facing corner. FA unknown.

40d. ★ A couple of face moves (from the top of the first section of crack) make for a shortcut to the mantel. FA unknown.

Jim Tobish leading T-Crack.
Photo: Tim Brown
(Also see photo on page 27)

41
Jonathan
5.11TR

Several feet to the right of the base of *T-Crack*, climb up past the obvious two inch edge on the overhanging face. FTR Jon Goodman, 1989.

42
David
5.11TR

Face moves ten feet to the right of *Jonathan*. A crucial bucket has since broken off, leaving the line unrepeated. FTR Dave Griffith, 1989.

43
Flakes Off
5.10TR

Between the base of the *Northwest Corner* and the beginning of *Any Minute Now*, a series of difficult, opposition moves lead over a horn to the first bolt on the *Any Minute Now* route. FTR Amos Clifford, mid-1970's.

44
Mirror in the
Bathroom
5.10+/A2

Just to the right of the base of the *Northwest Corner* route, aid climb the crack and roof leading out to the right. A short section of moderate fifth class climbing ends at a ledge and the first bolt on the *Any Minute Now* route. Aid and free-climb up and right, past bolts, to a belay atop a loose pillar. From the pillar climb up to the triple bolt belay for *Self Reflection*. A bolt up and right protects face moves on the left side of the main arete (5.10+). FA Curt Dixon and Warren Edgbert, 1980.

45
Self Reflection
★ ★ ★ 5.11b

Traverse, rappel, or climb up to the obvious horizontal ledge/crack three quarters up the left side of the main arete. There is a three bolt belay station. Utilizing thin sharp edges, head up and left past three bolts to the summit. The crux lies just above the second bolt. FA Kevin Brown and Mitch Jan, 1987.

46
Any Minute Now
★ ★ 5.6

Climb the cracks and loose slabs under the left-hand side of the large roof described below in *The Nose* route. Once under the roof, traverse left and around the corner to a bolt. Friction up a short ramp to the left. Keep traversing left to the corner and climb up to the Peanut Gallery. A classic hand-traverse (or 5.8 walk) leads out to the right using the horizontal crack. Once the alcove is attained, climb directly up the chimney/crack. FA (complete route) Amos Clifford and Joe Roland, 1973.

It is not known who first climbed individual portions of the route. During the fifties Mike Loughlin, John Cross, and Herbert Rickert were all known to have climbed the upper section beginning with the hand traverse from the Peanut Gallery.

Self Reflection: *Sylvia Mireles at the crux.* Photo: Kevin Steele

46a. Traverse directly out to the right from the alcove. After about 15 feet, and before the triple belay bolts, a shallow crack (5.7) leads up to dirty edges and the top. FA unknown.

47
The Nose
★ ★ ★ **5.11a**

There was a period of time around the mid-1970's that a group of locals, not knowing of any previous free ascents, led Henry Barber to think he had done the first free ascent of this route. In actuality, he was probably the first to free climb the Nose on-sight. Barber named his "new route" Euell (You'll) Gibbon. This name stuck for a short while, but the more commonly used "Nose" label prevailed. What Barber hadn't known was that the route had previously been led free several years earlier.

From under the large ceiling below the southwest corner, follow the crack leading up and over the center of the roof. Above this overhang, follow the crack to a ledge. Continue directly to the top via easier but runout face climbing. A variation to this roof problem is to face climb over the upper lip once you're about three quarters the way up the crack. FA Herbert Rickert 1960 (via direct aid). FFA unknown (either by Dave Black, Jim Donini, or Steve Gerdson), between 1970 and 1973.

Opposite: Kevin Steele leading The Nose. *Photo: Christopher Gardner*

Above: A Santa Barbara classic— Jon Goodman on The Nose. *Photo: Pat Briggs*

48
Smooth Arete
5.12

This route uses hand holds on the overhanging arete directly below and left of the overhanging crack at the beginning of *The Nose*. FTR Scott Cosgrove and Dave Griffith, fall of 1986.

49
Klingon
★★ 5.8

Beginning at the same point as the *The Nose* route, bypass the overhang via one of two variations. Either start directly from inside the alcove at the start of *The Nose* crack and head up and right, or start at a bush several feet right of the alcove and head up a shallow dihedral. Once out from under the roof area, continue up and right to a left-facing corner with a small ceiling above. Climb up under the ceiling and undercling out to the left. Using face holds (5.8) pull up to the ledge. Face moves lead more or less straight up from here to the top. FTR Unknown, pre-1960.

During the fifties climbers often bypassed the overhanging start of the Nose via the first part of Klingon. By doing a tension traverse (or pendulum) to the lip of the roof they gained access to the upper portions of the Nose route.

50
Mid-Face
★★★ 5.5-5.6

Climb the first section of *The Ladder* route to the large ledge. Traverse left about fifteen feet and by way of cracks, wander up and left to the top. FA Unknown, pre-1960.

51
The Ladder
★★ 5.3-5.5

This is most likely the very first route to be both top-roped as well as led in the tri-counties. For a short time, during the mid-1950's, the route was fixed with pitons so that climbers could lead it without having to repeatedly place and remove the protection. This and the Mid-Face route have probably seen more ascents than any other climbs in the area.

Follow the obvious crack at the base of the south face. The first ten feet are the crux, even if you bypass the difficult overhanging start. From the ledge halfway up the wall, either climb straight up a crack over a bulge (moderate fifth class), or traverse right a few feet and continue up easy rock to the top. FA Herbert Rickert, 1954.

52
Sleeper
5.10+

When walking down the trail to the base of the south face, keep looking above you for a short, overhanging thin crack about 10 feet in length. FA unknown, pre-1975 (possibly by Brian Smith).

Pat Briggs sticking to Smooth Arete. *Photo: Tim Brown*

Gibraltar Rock area (viewed from Gibraltar Road)

Gibraltar Rock Area

Gibraltar Road

53
La Escuela
5.10c/d TR

(aka: Hole Shot Roof) This is the tower that stands across the canyon just downhill from the large hairpin turn in Gibraltar Road. This is actually the upper part of Sycamore Canyon. The best approach is by walking down the fire road that begins at the hairpin turn. Climb directly up to, then over the center of the obvious roof. FTR Brian Smith and Dana Geary, 1975.

54
Sofa Master
5.7

Located on a shattered road cut about halfway between the start of Gibraltar Road and Gibraltar Rock. Look on the left-hand side of the road a few hundred feet down from a well-built stone and iron gate. Ascend the short S-shaped finger and hand crack that faces north.
FA Louis Andaloro and Rob Shreiber, 1980's.

Note: If this is your first look at a local climb, don't disparage, it gets a little better up the road in the Gibraltar Rock area.

Hole-in-the-Rock

This 30 foot high boulder stands across the road, to the east of Gibraltar Rock. The north, west, and south sides of the boulder offer good boulder and top-roped moves. The west face is punctuated by a hole halfway up the right-hand side.

55
Jump Back
★ ★ B/5.10+

Between *The Slant* and the left-hand edge of the north side, climb the overhanging face, via flakes and edges, to a small mantel ledge. Above the mantel, the angle eases.
FA Doug Hsu, pre-1980.

When first trying this route, Hsu took a flying leap backwards into the bushes after popping off of the crux moves.

56
The Slant
Moderate 5th

On the north side (facing the mountains) a shelf and crack extend diagonally up and left (awkward) in the middle of that face. FA unknown, pre-1975.

57
The Edge
★ **5.11c TR**

This is the sharp, clean arete forming the northwest corner of the boulder. Start the route atop the large blocks on the north side of the arete. FTR Kevin Brown and Tim Loughlin, 1977.

58
Left of the Hole
★ ★ **5.10+ TR**

As in the *Corner Pocket* route, climb into the hole. One move above the hole, traverse directly left until under the rock at the top. Climb to the top. FTR Steve Gerdson, pre-1975.

59
Corner Pocket
★ ★ **5.8 TR**

On the west side, climb the right-hand corner into the hole. From the hole, continue directly up the arete to the top. A variation is to climb directly to the top (5.9) not using the corner on the upper half. FTR unknown, pre-1975.

60
Well Hung
★ ★ **5.8-5.10 TR**

On the ocean side of the rock, the left-hand corner leads up to a small undercling. Using the arete makes for a nice 5.8. Without using the arete on the left, either climb directly up (5.10) or step to the right and up (easier). FTR Amos Clifford, pre-1975.

61
Center Peace
★ ★ **5.2**

Climb the easy moves up the center of the south face (ocean side) of the rock. The route diagonals slightly to the right. FA unknown, pre-1975.

62
Peace Work
5.10+ TR

On the right-hand side of the same wall as *Well Hung*, small edges lie between an "off-route" hole and the extreme right edge of the rock. FTR unknown, pre-1975.

Cig-Arete

63
Cig-Arete
5.11 TR

Walk a short distance up the path above Hole-In-The-Rock. Anchor bolts can be seen just off the trail to the right on a flat rock shelf at the edge of the drop-off to the road below. Rappel from the bolts to top-rope the overhanging arete.
FTR Craig Delbrook and Pat Briggs, 1989.

Doug Hsu heading into the crux of Jump Back. *Photo: Gary Tabor*

Gibraltar Gully

The following routes lie on individual rocks and faces in the gully directly below Gibraltar Rock itself. The gully is easily identified by all of the wrecked autos in it.

Lunch Rock: This is the large 40 foot high "boulder" that sits next to the road 30 feet or so down from Gibraltar Rock. You can easily walk out on top of it and see people climbing the south face of Gibraltar or look down the gully below to see *Crank Start.*

There are several top-rope possibilities below on Lunch Rock's southwest face. These include a large overhang with difficulties in the 5.10+ to 5.11 range, as well as moderately rated steep face climbing. The moderate routes were top-roped prior to 1980 but it is assumed that the first top-roped ascents of the more difficult overhang area were by Dave Griffith and Tony Becchio in late 1991.

A top-rope anchor can be easily set up off of vegetation or even your car.

64
Inner Tube Toes
5.10a TR

Approximately 50 feet down the road towards the Bolt Ladder area from Gibraltar Rock, and on the downhill (south) side of the road itself, sits a moderately sized rock with a sharp overhanging arete. Look for a bolt with no hanger.
FTR Kevin Brown and Jeff Smith, 1976.

65
T.R.'s TR
5th TR

A right-facing corner forms the left side of this triangular shaped slab, which lies just over the southerly edge of the flat area at the base of Gibraltar's south face. Rappel down to the base of the 40 foot high wall or scramble up from the gully near the base of *Crank Start*. The more you avoid using holds at either side of the slab, the harder the climbing.
FTR Terry Roland and Steve Tucker, spring 1991.

66
Crank Start
★★5.11

Overhanging bolted face in the gully below the South Face of Gibraltar. The climb rises from the debris of cars and trashed motorcycles. *The route was named for the hand-crank-started car wreck nearby.* FA Dave Griffith, Pat Briggs, and Tony Becchio, 1990.

67
Crank This
5.11d

After clipping the first three bolts of *Crank Start,* head off to the right past two bolts. Finish at a two bolt chain anchor.
FA John Perlin and Sean Mayes, May 1992.

The Bolt
Ladder Area

This formation is marked by the line of bolts leading up the yellowish roadcut a few hundred feet down the road from Gibraltar Rock. The lower part of the cliff is actually a roadcut, while the upper sections are still the original natural rock face.

If you want to set up a top-rope for the cliff, you'll need to scramble up the rock slab and bushy ridge just around the corner up the road towards Gibraltar Rock.

68
The Bolt Ladder
A1

Put up as a practice aid route for Sierra Club climbing classes. It is advisable to test each bolt before use, since the route sees numerous ascents. FA Tim McMahan and Bill Bancroft, 1969.

68a. The Bolt Ladder (Free) 5.10 ★ ★ Besides their utility for practicing aid climbing, this line of bolts also provides protection for a good face climb. Begin just left of the first bolt, following a small ramp up and right. Wander up the face following the bolts as closely as possible. Some 30 feet from the top, either head directly up (5.10), or traverse off to either side (5.9). Note: the climbing can approach 5.11 in difficulty if you follow the bolts closely. Several top-rope variations exist.
FFA Steve Gerdson, 1975.

68b. California Flake (Moderate 5th class): A few feet right of the start of the *Bolt Ladder* a small, right-facing corner heads up and right. This popular direct start variation connects up with the middle portion of the *Bolt Ladder* route. The route is named after the thin flake/plate that is encountered just above the point where the corner joins the line of bolts.
FA Unknown, pre-1980.

69
Finger Cracks
5.10a/b

Twenty feet to the right of the *Bolt Ladder* is a short finger crack basically leading nowhere.
FA Unknown, pre-1980.

Kevin Brown locked into the Finger Cracks, *Bolt Ladder Wall. Photo: Jeff Christianson*

The following route ascends the center of the rust-colored slab directly above the *Bolt Ladder* route. Approach is via the same ridge to the top of the *Bolt Ladder.*

70
Sweating Buckets
★★**5.11c**

At the end of a thin crack diagonal right past a sequence of difficult, bolt protected face moves. Take along pro for the initial crack. FA Dave Griffith and Pat Briggs, 1991.

Opposite:
Dave Griffith on
first ascent of
Sweating Buckets.
Photo: Tim Brown

Toxic Waste Wall

About 100 feet to the right of the *Bolt Ladder* route an orange colored wall diagonals up the slope towards Upper Gibraltar. Climb the steep path along the base of the wall.

71
Toxic Socks
5.9+

This is the left-hand route that ascends a seam fairly directly to the top. Five bolts protect the route plus a double bolt top anchor. FA Pat Briggs and Dave Griffith, November 21, 1991.

72
Hazardous Waste
★★ 5.10a (R)

A seam and small rib of reddish rock diagonal up the center of the cleanest section of rock. There are four protection bolts along with a double bolt anchor at the top.
FA Pat Briggs and Tony Becchio, October 28, 1991.

73
Chemical Warfare
5.10b

Thirty feet uphill from the start of *Hazardous Waste* is a vertical strip of dark colored rock with a seam/crack. Climb straight up past four bolts. Take along small to medium sized pro.
FA Pat Briggs and Tony Becchio, November 12, 1991.

74
Two Stone Wipe
5.9

This is the seam/crack between *Chemical Warfare* and *The Crockostimpy*. Bring your own pro.
FA Tim Brown, Pat Briggs, and Tony Becchio, Summer 1992.

75
The Crockostimpy
5.9

This route starts near the base of a tree about 150 feet right of *Chemical Warfare*. Climb on loose holds past three bolts. There is a double bolt anchor at the top. Pro was placed on lead.
FA Pat Briggs and Tim Brown, May 1992.

76
Stimpy on Crack
5.8

Climb past buckets to the crack leading to the top of *The Crockostimpy*. Pro: thin to 3 inch.
FA Tony Becchio, May 1992.

77
Solo One
5.7

Several feet to the right of *Stimpy On Crack* follow buckets directly to the top. About 20 feet in length, dirty and loose.
FA Pat Briggs, free solo, May 1992.

78
Solo Two
5.7

Ascend double cracks ten feet uphill from *Solo One*. A clean route. FA Tony Becchio, free solo, May 1992.

Upper Gibraltar

One tenth of a mile down the road from Gibraltar Rock, Upper Gibraltar can be seen on the upper left-hand side of the wash above the road. To reach the formation, park at Gibraltar Rock and head up the trail past Hole-in-the-Rock boulder. Continue following the trail up the ridge until you've reached the old fire road. Walk down to the top of Upper Gibraltar. The base of the rock is easily reached by hiking down and left (or rappelling). You can also approach from a trail starting at the base of the the Toxic Waste Wall. *Pseudomania, Gold Coin,* and *Try Something New* routes are best approached by traversing along the top of the main formation.

For several years during the 1970's word spread that one of the best climbs in the area was The Crescent. People seemed to be showing up from out of town interested only in doing this particular route. It didn't take them long to realize that, although it is a nice climb, it wasn't all that rumors had it cracked up to be.

79
Pseudomania
★ ★ ★ **5.11-**

(aka: Sterling Crack) Fifty feet to the left of the main face of Upper Gibraltar Rock is a broken, overhanging wall. Ascend the short, overhanging crack in the obvious right facing corner. Start the route by rappelling to the pedestal/ledge partway up the face (preferred); or scramble down the ridge to the west to the base of the wall. FTR Sterling Wilson, April 1987. FA David Griffith, April 1987, on sight.

80
Gold Coin
5.11a TR

Starting from the same pedestal as *Pseudomania*, this is the series of flakes and corners that lie just right of *Pseudomania*. Hard lieback moves lead to the crux move over a bulge. FTR Kevin Brown, Menzo Baird, and Chuck Fitch, 1987.

81
Try Something New
5.11+/5.12 TR

Climb the overhanging face 25 feet right of *Pseudomania*. There are three belay bolts at the top. FTR Hans Florine, Phil Requist, Leif Johnson, and Ted Pederson, Spring 1987.

Sterling Wilson on
Pseudomania.
Photo: Pat Briggs

The following routes lie on the main wall of Upper Gibraltar.

82
Dazed and Confused
5.10b

Climb the first section of *Triple Overhang* to the ledge. Climb straight up the face above, connecting briefly with *The Crescent* then moving left. Climb the arete directly to the top.
FA Steve Edwards, Mike Brown, and Jeff Buhl, December 1993.

83
A Route Runs
Through It
5.10+

Climb the first bulge of *Triple Overhang* (bolts have been added to this section). Climb the face between *Crescent* and *Triple Overhang*, past six bolts. FA Jeff Buhl and Mike Brown, spring 1993.

84
Triple Overhang
★ 5.6

At the lower left-hand side of the main face, a crack leads up and around a chockstone. Traverse right on the ledge to below a bulge. Climb the right-hand crack. Finish via fourth class to the left or continue up and right (5.6) on face holds to the top.
FTR Herbert Rickert et al., late 1950's. FA unknown.

85
The Crescent
★ ★ 5.7

The crescent shaped crack on the upper left-hand face of this formation was originally climbed via the first half of the *Triple Overhang* route. This way of climbing the Crescent bypasses the more difficult *Crescent Direct* route.
FA unknown, prior to the *Crescent Direct*.

86
The Crescent
Direct
5.8

Thirty feet up the slope to the right of the beginning of the *Triple Overhang* route, climb directly (5.8) to where two cracks split a bulge. Negotiate the bulge by way of the left-leaning crack. Continue using the crack until it is possible to top-out by either way mentioned in the finish of the *Triple Overhang* route.
FA Joe Roland and Amos Clifford, early 1970's.

87
The Soul
5.11b

Starts thirty feet uphill from the start of *Crescent Direct*. Move left, then head directly up the face directly between *Triple Overhang* and the next seam/crack to the right. Eight bolts protect the upper half of the climb.
FA Jeff Buhl and Mike Brown, spring 1993.

87a. The Gibbon, 5.10-: From the main horizontal break partway up *The Soul*, traverse right 8 feet to a bolt. Climb a bulge then a seam/crack past 7 bolts. Connect with *The Soul*.

88
Right Routes
Mid-5th Class

The line on the topo was climbed by Jeff Buhl in 1993. Dave Oates and Amos Clifford top-roped several other routes between it and route 87 in 1975.

Upper Gibraltar Gully

89
V-ger
5.7

This climb sits on the hillside above the main gully above Gibraltar Rock. Walk up the ridge on the north (left) side of the gully. The V-ger rock is spotted as having a sloping, grey face leading up to an overhang. From the east (right) side of the rock, step across a chimney and out onto a ledge. From the ledge, climb face moves to the overhang, then up and left to the top. This area holds potential for more routes.
FA Doug Hsu and Steve Tucker, December 1979.

From the old fire road on the approach to Cold Springs Dome, you can get a good view of the upper portions of Gibraltar Gully. Across the way lies an orangeish slab which is best approached by following the fire road around the top of the gully. The following routes ascend this unspectacular slab.

90
Leftover
5.7

On the left-hand side of the slab, boulder moves from a leaning rock get you onto the face. The route ends at a boulder at the top. FA Mike Forkash and Gary Anderson, late 1970's.

91
Virgin Territory
5.8

Starting at the lower, right-hand side of the slab, diagonal up and left to the end of the Leftover route. The route is partially protected by a bolt.
FA Gary Anderson and Mike Forkash, late 1970's.

Lower Gibraltar

Lower Gibraltar consists of a half dozen routes on a small crag west of Gibraltar Rock. Park at the pulloff at the second right-hand turn, uproad from Gibraltar Rock. Walk down a trail leading out onto a small ridgetop. Wander down and right along the ridge 100 feet or so to the top of the Lower Gibraltar formation. The base of the formation is reached by scrambling down around either side of the face (or rappelling).

The original route climbed here was Chimney Sweep, but the first attempts on Lieback Annie caught people's attention with many climbers falling from the awkward mantel near the top.

92
Lieback Annie
★ ★ ★ 5.7

Around the corner to the left of *Chimney Sweep*, climb up a short ramp into a left-facing dihedral. Near the top, an awkward mantel from a layback makes the route very enjoyable.
FA Curt Dixon, Brett Ballinger and Tom Adam, October 1977.

Curt Dixon on the first ascent of Lieback Annie. Photo: Bob Granett

93
Chimney Sweep
5.8

Ascend the crack/chimney running up the middle of the face. FA Curt Dixon and Warren Edgebert, fall 1977.

94
Thin Cracks
5.9

To the right of *Chimney Sweep* and a few feet to the right of a right-facing corner, ascend cracks and face holds to easier climbing. A short unappealing route.
FA Curt Dixon, Warren Edgebert, and Tom Adam, 1977.

95
Conundrum
5.8

Climb the face just left of *Lieback Annie*. Follow the thin crack on the upper face to the top. Pitons were used on the first ascent for protection. There were originally no bolts on the route, which made the first half significantly more sporting.
FA Bruce Hendricks and Bruce Watts, September 1982.

The following route, easily visible from the Peanut Gallery Ledge on Gibraltar Rock, is best approached from the small ridgetop mentioned on the approach to Lower Gibraltar. Scramble or rappel to the base.

96
Warrior Crack
5.10c

This route lies on the small buttress directly across the creek to the west of Gibraltar Rock. A bolt protects the crux leading to a small hand crack. If the route hasn't seen much activity, it may be wise to first clean the dirt funneling down from the top. FA Kevin Brown, Butch Grosvener, Menzo Baird, 1986.

Phantom Rock

Park at the next major parking turn-off up Gibraltar Road from Lower Gibraltar's parking spot. Head down the ridge to the west towards the canyon. To reach the base of the formation, descend either of the following ways:

Follow the path of least resistance down and left to the top of the main body of rock. There are several medium sized Manzanita bushes near the drop-off. From here it is easiest to rappel to the bottom then scramble down towards the large oak tree.

The other way is to continue straight down the main ridgeline then angling down and right around the backside of the formation. This involves some fourth class scrambling. Follow the base of the rock around to the large oak tree.

There are bolt anchors at the top for belays. All the routes can be top-roped. There are additional top-ropes to the right of the *South Face* route.

97
Scorpion Exile
★ 5.10a

From the large oak tree, climb the obvious dihedral above. Two bolts and placing a medium sized stopper will get you to the roof. Turn the roof on its left side and continue on good rock past two more bolts to the top. FA Dave Griffith, Pat Briggs, Tony Becchio, and Jim Tobish, 1992.

98
South Face
5.8 TR

Climb the obvious two inch wide crack that heads up and left. Move into the large hole then head right and up to the top. As of this writing there are still some loose flakes to contend with as well as a loose block near the top belay anchor bolts. FTR Chuck Ford, 1981.

The Tombstone

This is the obvious pillar visible across Rattlesnake Canyon from Gibraltar Rock. Approach from the base of Phantom Pinnacle. Wander downhill into the creekbed on a very faint trail. Follow the creek downstream until it is possible to head up the slope to the base of the Tombstone. An alternate approach is via the same creekbed, but coming from below and branching off from the Rattlesnake Trail. Either way is a bit of a bushwag.

99
Chim Knee
5.2

This is the easy slot up the left (south) side of the rock. FA Pat Briggs, 1985.

100
Don't Fret Arete
5.10

Climb the obvious flakes on the southeast arete. FA Kevin Brown and Menzo Baird, October 1985.

101
Stormbringer
★★★ 5.11+

Start climbing from the small pedestal at the base of the east face. Follow the small crack that heads up and left. After the crack ends, continue on face moves keeping to the right of the arete. The route is protected by five bolts. Quality rock and route. FA Tony Becchio, Dave Griffith, and Pat Briggs, February 1992. (See photo, next page.)

102
Death of a Salesman
★ 5.8+

Wide crack on right side of the east face. Take caution with loose rock. FA Kevin Brown and Menzo Baird, October 1985.

Two top-rope problems lay on the short orange colored wall up the canyon from the Tombstone. The crag actually sits on the hillside below the switchbacks of Gibraltar Road across the canyon to the west from Upper Gibraltar Rock. Approach is down a steep scree chute from the road.

103
Left Crack
5.9 TR

Left-most of two cracks. FTR John Perlin and Dave Jelnick, 1990.

104
Lurk Between the Lines 5.10a TR

Right-hand of two cracks. FTR John Perlin and Dave Jelnick, 1990.

*Dave Griffith on
first ascent of* Stormbringer.
Photo by Pat Briggs

Cold Springs Dome

> *"...you'll laugh so hard,*
> *your sides will ache,*
> *your heart will go pitter-pat..."*
>
> —*from Felix The Cat cartoon theme song.*

Located in the upper reaches of the west fork of Cold Springs Canyon, these 60 to 130 foot faces are characterized as very challenging climbing. "The Dome" was originally discovered for its climbing potential by Amos Clifford in 1974 .

Cold Springs Dome can be a good place to climb on hot days since many of the routes are in the shade for most of the day.

The twenty minute approach begins at the parking turnoffs at Gibraltar Rock and heads up the ridge to the east, past Hole-in-the-Rock boulder. Follow a small trail up the ridge to an old, over-grown fire road. Continue left, on the north side of the ridge, to a point approximately 150 yards up the fire road. Where this road takes a slight dip down, turn right. A small ridge and trail lead down to the formation.

The base of the principal faces can be reached by scrambling down along the base of the east side of the hill. Bolts have been placed at various spots along the tops of the walls for top-rope belays. It is possible to access the belay bolts for the *Makunaima* wall by scrambling and climbing up (or down) the right side of the south face. This, however, entails some exposed third and fourth-class climbing.

The formation is probably best known for being home to one of Santa Barbara's true classics, *Makunaima*.

105 **Get-da-Lead Out** **5.8**	On the lower south face of the Dome, this route passes through several bolts and bulges on loose rock. FA Mike Forkash and Gary Anderson, 1980.

106
Anasazi
5.10b TR

Ascends a lie-back flake left of *Makunaima*. There are two bolts at the top for a top-rope anchor.
FTR Cliff Tillotson et al., 1988.

107
No Woman No Cats
★★ **5.11b TR**

Climb the face just left of *Makunaima,* through the large dishes.
FTR Phil Requist and Hans Florine, 1987.

108
Makunaima
★★★ **5.11c**

(aka: Calamity Jam) *From the first time anyone saw this route it has been recognized as a classic. Because of this, many people, including the likes of Henry Barber and Jeff Lowe, gave it a serious look. Not until after the line had seen a number of direct-aid, as well as top-roped free ascents, was the route finally climbed free on lead. Makunaima, pronounced Mah-ku-nah-EE-mah, came from a character in an old movie. This route appears on the cover of this book.*

Climb the obvious crack that diagonals up the middle of the overhanging southeast face. Two crux sections of finger jamming lie beyond the horn. Traverse off to the left after the second crux. FA Rick Mosher et al., via direct-aid, 1975. FTR (free) Bill Puttnam, 1976. FFA Mike Forkash and Alan Wolman, 1980.

108a. Jericho Dude 5.11+ TR: Climb straight up the face, staying right of the large holes and pockets. Follow a small rib through a shallow pocket and small edges. Connect with the standard *Makunaima* route at the point where the main crack doglegs from horizontal back to vertical.
FTR David Griffith, January 1991.

108b. Homo Erectus 5.11b TR: From the horn, continue directly straight up the face past a small roof.
FTR David Griffith, 1986.

108c. Direct Finish 5.11+ TR: Instead of traversing off to the left after the crux sections mentioned in *Makunaima,* continue straight up the line of weakness to the top. FTR approximately 1980. FA Brents Hawks.

109
Kneeanderthal
★★ **5.11d TR**

Climb *Makunaima* through the first crux to just under the next bulge. Using pockets and holes traverse twelve feet right under the small roof and into a series of flakes and pockets which follow a separate crack system. Follow these up for about 20 feet to the large horizontal hole below the big roof. Traverse left six feet under the roof. Pull over the roof on an obvious hold to the top.
FTR Phil Requist and Hans Florine, March 1986.

110
Predators Keep
the Balance
5.12a/b TR

(aka: Cro-Magnon) Climb the orange face just left of *Straw Dogs.* Finish over the roof via the *Kneeanderthal* finish to *Makunaima* or to the right, over the roof via pockets leading up and right. FTR Phil Requist, Kevin Steele, Dave Griffith, December, 1988. *An interesting historical note is that in the late 1970's Brian Smith gave this route it's original attempt on lead, without first working out the moves on a top-rope. He got as far as the roof where he took a bad fall and pendulumed into the Straw Dogs corner.*

111
Straw Dogs
5.9+

This route leads up the crack in the corner formed by the over-hanging east wall and the south-facing slab. Difficult lie-back-ing constitutes the crux section. FA Steve Fitch and Chuck Fitch, February 1975.

112
Baby Scorpions
5.10c

Climb obvious buckets about 10 feet right of *Straw Dogs.* The route is about 25 feet in length and pretty much follows the arete on the large blocky buttress. FTR Phil Requist and Hans Florine, March 1988.

113
Rock Bottom
5.7

Follow the dirty crack just right of the *Straw Dogs* route to a ledge. From the ledge, swing left onto rotten face moves. Continue to the top. FA Amos Clifford, 1975.

114
Snidely's Whiplash
5.8

Climb the easy ledges and holes just to the right of *Rock Bottom* onto harder face moves leading to the main ledge midway up the rock. This route basically ascends the section between *Rock Bottom* and *Magic Bag.* FA Bruce Hendricks and K. Callaway, September 1983.

115
Magic Bag
★ ★ 5.9

Starting in the middle of the face between *Rock Bottom* and *Felix* climb directly up 30 feet to a bolt. Head up and left to a good stance and a second bolt. Climb up and right past a third bolt then around a small bulge to easier climbing and the large ledge halfway up the formation. Because of rope drag it is easiest to belay at the ledge. Climb over the obvious overhang (awkward) past a fixed piton overhead. Several zigzags up ramps, ledges, and corners lead to the top (protection was placed on lead). FA Steve Tucker, Dick Saum, and Chuck Fitch, 1981.

Dave Kelley on Master Cylinder.
Photo: Bruce Hendricks.

116
Felix
5.7

This was the first route climbed at the Dome. Directly above the large bush on the right side of the south-facing slab, follow a widening crack to the roof. Traverse left to a large ledge where it is usual to belay. Climb over the chockstone above the left-hand side of the ledge and head for the top via a right-facing corner. FA (first pitch only) Amos Clifford, Joe Roland, Chrys Mitchell, and Steve Tucker, 1974.
FA (complete route) John Tucker and Steve Tucker, 1974.

117
Master Cylinder
★ ★ ★ 5.9

Near the lower toe of the east face and just up the hill from the start of *Felix,* a thin crack ascends a steep section around a small corner to the right side of the main overhanging "prow." Lieback/jam the left side of the obvious flake/crack and face climb the wall above. The upper section is protected by two bolts.
FA Bruce Hendricks and Dave Kelley, May 1983.

The first ascent party led the top section of the route without being able to stop and place any protection. They later returned and placed the upper bolts via top-rope to protect what had been a very unwanted runout! When you're on this route, try imagining the lead without the bolts.

118
Cat Walk
5.7

Start from a small, left-sloping ledge, uphill and to the right of the start of *Master Cylinder.* Climb up over loose flakes to the right side of the prow. Hand-traverse (5.4) left under the prow, until you join up with the Felix route.
FA Steve Tucker and Amos Clifford, 1974.

119
Gypsy Moon
5.10d TR

This is the beautiful arete between *Master Cylinder* and *Post-Modern Retro-Classic.* No fixed top anchors; be creative.
FTR: Steve Edwards & Rob Norris, Spring 1992.

120
Post-Modern
Retro Classic
★ ★ 5.10b

This route lays in the middle of the steep, 60 foot high northeast face. Several bolts lead to a double bolt anchor at the top. A route easily set up as a top-rope. FTR Gary Anderson, 1980.
FA Rob Norris and Pat Briggs, May 1992.

Rattlesnake Canyon

A sandstone bridge on Las Canoas Road crosses over Rattlesnake Creek near the entrance to Skofield Park. Park close to the bridge and hike the trail (sometimes a dirt road) up the canyon.

Bridge Boulders

There is good bouldering near the bridge and just up the creek.

Grids and Squares

Just beyond the point where the trail reaches the dirt road there are rocks both uphill and downhill. The larger rock mass above the road usually calls for a top rope and offers both steep face climbing on its north (mountain) side as well as lower angle slab climbing on the side facing the dirt road (west). The boulder below the dirt road also calls for a top rope as a fall can lead to a bit of a tumble down the steep creek bed.

This area was first discovered for its climbing potential by Amos Clifford, who in the 1970's habitually wandered the chaparral in search of obscure climbing rocks and rare herbs. It is known as the "Zen Grids and Squares" area.

Rattlesnake Crags

Past the Grids and Squares rocks, follow the road and trail a couple of miles upstream beyond a stand of pines, to where the trail crosses the creek for the third time. The rocks surrounding this creek crossing have shown potential for new climbs. Note: It is also possible to reach this area by starting at the trailhead just down the road from Gibraltar Rock.

121
Fun in the Sun
★ 5.7

Twenty feet before the creek crossing, head up and left through brush and trees along the base of the rock wall. A gully heads for the most blank section of the upper headwall. The route ascends this headwall and is protected by bolts.
FA Mike Forkash and Gary Anderson, 1980.

122
Made in the Shade
★ 5.7

After making the creek crossing, a seam runs up the ocean side of a pedestal. From the top of the pedestal, face moves lead up and right to a walk-off to the right. Scramble back down to the creek. FA Gary Anderson and Mike Forkash, 1980.

Lower Mission Canyon

Drive up Mission Canyon Road towards the Botanic Garden. Turn left onto Tunnel Road and park at its end. Hike up the paved access road past the gate. At the last left-hand bend in the road before the bridge you will be able to get a good view of the rock faces across the canyon to the east. From this same bend in the road, a trail (often over-grown) diagonals down to the creek (you'll find a great swimming hole here). Head upstream until under the larger of the rock cliffs.

Several old pitons and bolts of unknown origin have been found in this area suggesting that ascents of these cliffs took place a number of years prior to the 1970's. One of these bolts is at the base of the arete, just left of the start to *Pin Tan Alley*. There is also a single bolt out on the face and just right of the *Pin Tan Alley* first pitch. No record of who placed them or what the routes may be has come to light.

A steep dirt and brush covered ramp leads up and left to the base of Pin Tan Alley. Further up this ramp a group of large ceilings split by cracks can be accessed. The larger of these roofs is loose and dirty. However, the area around *Blowin' Chunks* holds potential for further routes. An old sling around a small tree on one of the ledges suggests that attempts have been made at one of the cracks.

The face up the ramp to the left of *Blowin' Chunks* is a possibility for new routes but is a bit rotten.

123
Pin Tan Alley
5.7/A2

Not too far up the dirt ramp under the main cliff face, and just past the first cave at the base of that wall, a bolt (not the ancient bent-over bolt) marks the beginning of the route. A lieback/reach is necessary to clip the first bolt. Aid climb a couple of fixed pins leading to a right leaning crack and seam. Follow this seam up and right until it intersects a steep gully. Belay in the gully. Traverse left, out across a poorly protected face, then up to a ledge on the arete. Because of rope drag, you may want to belay here. Climb up and right across steeper rock. Either climb straight up the middle overhang via a slot/crack (5.8), or traverse further around to the right (5.7) and up to the top. Since its first ascent the first pitch has sprouted a few additional fixed pins. FA Steve Tucker and Chuck Fitch, 1981.

On one of the first attempts to climb Pin Tan Alley, *Bruce Hendricks was aid climbing the beginning of the first pitch. The first bolt on the route had been put in "just in case". When Hendricks was several placements above the bolt, the camming unit he was standing on blew out and Bruce went flying. The "just in case" bolt stopped his head-first fall only a couple of feet off the ground.*

124
Blowin' Chunks
5.9

Climb up under the roofs to a lieback crack that leads up and to the left. The initial part of this section goes at 5.7, but the angle soon steepens (5.9) and the climb becomes dirtier. Take medium to large pro. FA Curt Dixon and Warren Edgebert, 1979.

125
Top Rock
5.8

On the creek side of the large boulder sitting atop the main cliffs, ascend the corner containing a lieback crack and loose flake. The top moves of this route are protected by bolts. FA Rick Mosher et al., late 1970's.

Seven Falls

The access road from the top of Tunnel Road passes over a bridge. It then winds its way around a hill where it not only turns into a dirt road but forks in two directions. Take the left-hand fork up the hill. Instead of following the trail signs up Tunnel Trail to Camino Cielo, continue on the dirt road until it narrows down to a trail. This is the Jesusita Trail. Follow the trail down to the creek crossing. Follow the creek up to the pools and cascades of Seven Falls.

Lower Theology Crag

Actually a large boulder, this rock is located on the right-hand side of the creek upstream from the trail/creek crossing and before you reach Seven Falls.

126
Leviticus
A3

This is the obvious overhanging dihedral and thin crack splitting the large boulder. FTR Kevin Brown, Jeff Christianson, 1987.

127
Holy Grail
5.10a

Fifteen feet to the right of *Leviticus* is another dihedral with a tree at its base. A fist crack leads to a small roof and the crux. FA Kevin Brown, Jeff Christianson, 1987.

Upper Theology Crag

This formation lies above the water falls and pools of Seven Falls. A bit of steep scrambling, bushwhacking, and even getting wet may be necessary to get past the falls. This is the a large formation with the inscription "Old Mission To Study Philosophy And Theology" at its base.

128
Fire From Within
★ ★ 5.11a TR

Starting on the north face, a large black water groove marks the beginning of strenuous face climbing. Five bolts. FTR Menzo Baird, Marty Snyder, 1987.

129
Beggar's Banquet
★★ 5.11b

Arete to the left of *Trial of Faith*. Move left onto face for last twenty feet. Crux just before last bolt. Eight bolts. 65 feet. Triple bolt anchor on top. FA Stuart Ruckman, spring 1993.

130
Trial of Faith
5.10d TR

An overhanging wall starts at the inscribed rock. Climb up to a wide crack which tapers to fingers. As of this writing the route does not continue beyond the end of the crack (the top is an elusive 20 feet further). FTR Menzo Baird, Kevin Brown, 1987.

131
Trouble with
Normal
★ 5.11a

(aka: Triple Threat Arete) Stemming and lie-backing lead up inside corner just right of *Trial of Faith*. Be careful with the beautiful weathered sandstone features. Move right, out onto arete, bear-hugging the arete itself. Seven bolts. Crux is below last bolt. Double bolt anchor on top.
FTR Dave Griffith, Hans Florine and Jon Goodman, 1988.
FA Stuart Ruckman, spring 1993.

Upper Mission Canyon

To reach the Tower of Doom, Upper Mission Waterfall, Upper Mission Slabs, and Twenty Years After, hike down the Tunnel Trail from East Camino Cielo (about 20 minutes). Map, p. 119.

Twenty Years After

As you round the corner in the trail and get your first full view of the Upper Mission Slabs area look for a solitary, pointed, light-colored boulder. It lies partway up a small ridge between the creek bed on your left and the main rock outcrops to the right. Approach up the creekbed from the trail for a couple hundred yards. From the cascade with a large overhung boulder on the left, scramble up the brushy hillside on the right (east).

132
Trompe L'oeil
5.10+ TR

From atop the obvious platform climb the slightly overhanging pocketed west face, left of center.
FTR Steve Tucker, March 1992.

133
Fools Progress
5.9 TR

This is the prominent, narrow, dished trough seen from the trail that runs up the center (south edge) of the rock.
FTR Bruce Watts, March 1992.

134
More My Speed
5.7 TR

Head straight up the left side of the south facing slab (just right of *Fools Progress*).
FTR Amos Clifford, March 1992.

Tower of Doom

From the trail, when standing on top of Upper Mission Falls, the "Tower" can be seen down and to the east (right). Continue down the trail for about a hundred feet further until you find a faint path heading down the gully along the base of the waterfall. You'll know you're on the right track if you end up traversing down along a ledge to the left-hand base of the *Waterfall Face*. Head down the creekbed a short way to reach the Tower. Scramble up either side of the Tower to any of the faces.

Routes are listed from south to north (left to right as faced from the creekbed).

Tower of Doom
Photo: Tim Murphy

135	This route is the best way to gain the top of the formation in
Hot Steps	order to set up top rope anchors. From the uphill side, climb
5.0 (no pro)	the right-hand edge of the short west face (easy but exposed).
	FA Unknown.

136	Climb the center of the South Face past a small right-facing
Elfin Edges	corner.
5.10c TR	FTR Jim Tobish.

137
Flakes of Doom
5.10+ TR
Ascend the right side of the South Face, keeping left of the arete. The name speaks for itself. FTR Jim Tobish.

138
Changing of the Guard 5.10+ TR
Ascend the southeast arete, often staying right of the corner. FTR Jim Tobish.

139
Tears to the Eyes
5.10b TR
Start in the middle of the east face, head up and right. Climb as much as possible out over the center of the largest overhang at the top. FTR Warren Gibbs.

140
Edge of Darkside
5.10 TR
Follow the right hand edge of the East Face. FTR Warren Gibbs and Jim Tobish.

141
Hanging in the Dark 5.11 TR
Climb the right edge of the North Face. FTR Steve LaFluer.

Upper Mission Waterfall

Follow the same approach for reaching the Tower of Doom. There is a point where Tunnel Trail jogs at the brink of the Waterfall Face. These routes lie directly below.

142
Waterfall Face
A3
Two direct-aid routes ascend the overhanging section at the top left section of the main waterfall course (up two parallel hairline cracks). Marginal A3 placements in rotten rock. FA Zolton Von Somogyi and Ted Stryker, 1987.

Upper Mission Slabs

These large slabs located directly above Tunnel Trail, at the top of Mission Canyon (above Tower of Doom and the waterfall) have been looked at by a number of people over the years. No known routes have been completed. These rocks are very prominent when viewed from Santa Barbara, and many climbers have reconnoitered the route possibilities.

There have been signs of attempts; old slings and second-hand stories. For example, Paul Corwin and Amos Clifford climbed several pitches in the fall of 1972, but described the rock as unpleasant and the route as vague and overvegetated.

East
Camino
Cielo

The drive along East Camino Cielo is one of the most spectacular in the tri-counties. The road closely follows the ridgeline of the Santa Ynez mountains for many miles before dropping down into the Mono basin of the upper Santa Ynez river.

On a clear day you can see the ocean sparkling out beyond the Channel Islands and see the backcountry peaks of the San Rafael mountains to the north. As you progress eastward, Gibraltar and Jameson lakes can be seen in the river valley below. To the south, on the ocean side of the ridge, you are passing by the upper headwaters of San Roque, Mission, Cold Springs, San Ysidro, and Romero canyons.

As you approach the vicinity of Hermit and Kryptor rocks keep an eye out for the section of road where you look south, down into San Ysidro Canyon. This is the only spot where both the Upper and Lower San Ysidro Canyon cliff faces can be seen at the same time.

The driveable part of East Camino Cielo eventually takes you near Jameson Lake and the Mono Debris Dam. Not too far up the road past Mono Dam are the Mono and Little Caliente Hot Springs which, if you know their whereabouts, can be a pleasant addition to the long drive.

Technically, East Camino Cielo continues further eastward, in bits and pieces of trail and/or fire road. It finally joins up with Highway 33 just north of Ojai near Matilija Hot Springs.

The following are those formations that can be accessed via the portion of East Camino Cielo between San Marcos Pass and Mono.

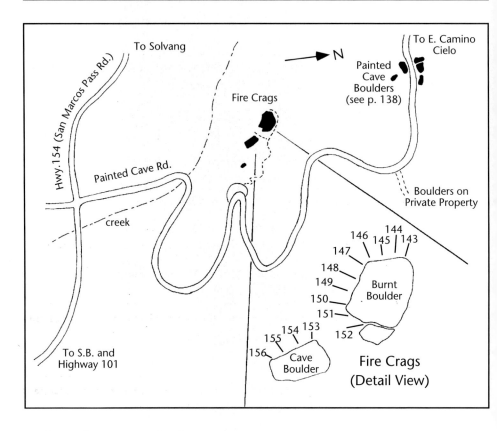

Map labels: To Solvang • To E. Camino Cielo • Painted Cave Boulders (see p. 138) • N • Fire Crags • Hwy-154 (San Marcos Pass Rd.) • Painted Cave Rd. • creek • Boulders on Private Property • To S.B. and Highway 101 • 146 147 148 149 150 151 152 153 154 155 156 • 144 145 143 • Burnt Boulder • Cave Boulder • Fire Crags (Detail View)

Painted Cave Road

Fire Crags

Visible uphill from the intersection of 154 and Painted Cave Road. Approach from pullout as displayed on the map (above). A trail leads from the pullout on the hairpin turn down and across to the top of the boulders, which are 20 to 40 feet tall and composed of very friable sandstone. Questionable alteration and drilling of holds has occurred here.

143
Europe Revisited
5.7

Two bolts on the far left.
FA Randy Judycki et. al., 1992.

144
Tester
5.9

Three bolts just to the right of *Europe Revisited*.
FA Randy Judycki et. al., 1992.

145
Short Shot
5.7

Directly through the cave at the left side of NW face of Burnt Boulder, to the top. FTR Brent Bain, Derek Jensen, Randy Judycki, Ryan Campbell, 1992.

146 **Bent Brain** **5.8**	From several feet right of the previous route, climb straight up past four bolts. FTR Brent Bain et. al., 1992.
147 **Jensen's Jugs** **5.10b**	Start at the left edge of the largest recess, climb up and left past four bolts through another recess. FTR Jensen et. al., 1992.
148 **Movin' Out** **5.11a/b**	Climb over tallest part of the largest recess and straight up past five bolts. FTR Judycki and Mike Colee, 1992.
149 **Grib Dat Hole** **5.11a**	Climb over the middle of the roof at the distinctive four-inch hole. Continue up through the holds (6 bolts). FTR Colee and Judycki, 1992.
150 **Finger Fit** **5.11b**	From the base of the large burnt tree at the right side of the large recess climb straight past 5 bolts. FTR Judycki and Colee, 1992.
151 **Face the Seam** **5.10**	On the ocean side (west face) of Burnt Boulder climb through the overlaps and into the groove/seam above. FTR Colee and Judycki, 1992.
152 **Black Crack** **5.9**	Climb the wide, black slot between the two boulders. FTR Colee and Judycki, 1992.
153 **Quick Crank** **5.10+**	Climb the left edge of the NW side of the Cave Boulder. FTR Judycki and Colee, 1992.
154 **reaming Knee Knee** **5.11b /c**	A few feet right of *Quick Crank,* climb directly through the hole to the top. Three bolts. FTR Colee and Judycki, 1992.
155 **3-F** **5.11d**	(aka: Flaccidly Flexing Forearms) Climb directly to the bolts at the top center of the face. FTR Judycki and Colee, 1992.
156 **Crack It Up** **5.9**	Climb up the right edge of the boulder. FTR Judycki, Campbell, 1992.

Painted Cave Cliff

Visible up the road from the Painted Cave Boulders and just before the Chumash Painted Cave State Historical Park. There are two routes that ascend the rock band directly beneath the homes.

The Painted Cave Boulders next to and overhanging the road are described in the Santa Barbara Bouldering section (pages 138-142).

Do Not climb on the rocks surrounding the Chumash Painted Cave State Historical Park.

Tor Archer and Jeff Schloss had just set up their belay anchors and started to climb. Suddenly, rocks started to fall from above. The rocks kept coming, and the two climbers couldn't figure out what was going on. They finally stepped away from the wall only to find that the source of the problem was a lady tossing the projectiles off the hillside above. The climbers yelled up to her that they would leave if only she would cease the bombardment. Surely, with such an intense barrage, she was trying to drive them off.

Upon seeing that someone was below her, the woman started to apologize profusely and was glad no one had been hit. She then proceeded to invite them to complete their task and come up for a visit.

When they reached the top of the climb she served them refreshments and explained that once a year she took time to clear her back yard of stones. The easiest way to get rid of the rocks was to simply toss them over the side of the cliff.

Talk about bad timing! The two climbers had picked the one day out of the year to do the ascent that the woman cleared her yard.

157
Writing on the Wall
5.10d

Approach is via a brush filled gully to the left side of the rock band. The route is the obvious thin hand crack cutting the roof just below a house. FA Tor Archer and Jeff Schloss, 1987.

158
Split Rock
5.10

On the extreme right-hand side of the cliff band and up a slope above a turn in the road lies a large separated rock split by a crack. The climb is short but enjoyable.
FA Amos Clifford, late 1970's.

Twin Piles

After driving 3.2 miles on East Camino Cielo from San Marcos Pass, the Twin Piles formation can be seen to the south. The approach begins three tenths of a mile past the mushroom-shaped water tank on the right. Park at the second "No Shooting" sign on the right. Hike towards the ocean, up and across the hill just ahead of the parking area. At the top center of the hill and near a large boulder, the trail (hard to find) to Twin Piles takes off through the brush. The approach takes about 20 minutes each way. While on the approach, the formations cannot be seen until about half way down the trail. The area can also be reached by driving up Painted Cave Road.

The West Faces of Twin Piles.

Kevin Brown Leading Tube Ride.
Photo: Mark Chun

Ascend the crack that appears at the end of the trail. FA Menzo Baird and Zolton Von Somogyi, December 19, 1987.

159
Menzonic Tremor
5.10b

To the west of *Menzonic Tremor*, ascend the crack past the overhang, then continue up the seam/ramp to the top. FA Ted Stryker, Z. Von Somogyi, Brian Wise, and Michele Hale, December 19, 1987.

160
Tube Ride
5.10b

Follow the line of five bolts (placed on lead) that lead up the prow of the larger formation. FA Zolton Von Somogyi and Ted Stryker, January 9, 1988.

161
Rats in the Cellar
5.10

La Cumbre Peak

There are several boulder problems around the summit.

162
Jumpin' Jive
5.10

Lies on the summit block on the ocean side of the boulder directly below the summit lookout tower. A short top-rope line ascends the southeast corner of the rock.
FTR Warren Gibbs, Pat Holt, and Bob Hass, 1987.

Earth Watch

The climbs lie about 150 feet directly downhill from the summit lookout tower. Approach by following the trail that wraps around the fenced summit tower area. The trail becomes faint, but the top of the outcrop (marked by bolts) is quickly reached. Rappel or scramble to the bottom. There is a chimney exit on the east end of the face.

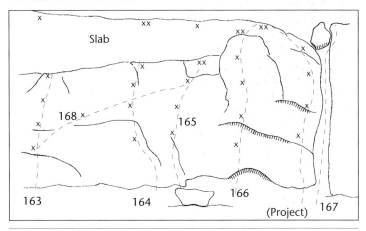

163
Clubbing Baby Seals
5.10b

The far left route on the face. Four bolts.
FA John Perlin and Viju Mathew, Spring 1992.

164
Project Earth Watch
5.11a

This is the original route at the outcrop. It lies in the center of the face. From the first bolt head up and left. The route leans to the right past two bolts.
FA John Perlin and Viju Mathew, January 1992.

165
Manhattan Project
5.11a

Starts right of *Project Earth Watch* and heads directly up past three bolts to a double bolt top anchor. The route is both the least steep and the loosest on the cliff.
FA John Perlin, Spring 1992.

166
Smear the Queer
5.12b

Four bolts with a flake on the left at half height.
FA John Perlin 1993.

167
Tankers in the Channel
Easy 5th

A chimney exit on the east end of the face.

168
Drift Net
5.11c

This contrived route traverses the entire wall from left to right. Connect the following bolts: first bolt of *Baby Seals*, to a separate bolt on the right; the second and third bolts on *Project Earth Watch;* the third bolt and finish on the top anchor of *Manhattan Project*. FA John Perlin, Spring 1992.

Cathedral Peak

The road leading off of East Camino Cielo to the La Cumbre Peak lookout forms a loop (a gate often blocks car access). Halfway up this, the road makes a sharp left turn. Here, a pull-out on the right begins the trek down and across to Cathedral Peak.

The hike takes at least 20 minutes one way. Before starting, it would be wise to survey the approach. although a new trail has recently been cut, it would be wise to wear long pants for protection from the inevitable encounters with dense and clutching chaparral.

Starting at the turnout, head toward the large boulders just down the hill. From these rocks start traversing down and right (west) following a poor trail. Continue this diagonal descent until you reach the ridge leading southward toward Cathedral Peak. Follow the ridge down via a marked trail to the low saddle.

From the saddle, head up and left. If you lose the trail, keep bushwhacking until you reach a rock headwall and the summit of Cathedral Peak.

To reach the base of the technical routes on the south side, scramble down and around the east side, following the base of the main rock mass. There is a register at the top of the formation.

Cathedral Peak

169
Cave Route
★ **5.5**

(aka: Les Caves) At the base of the rock is a large cave. A second, higher cave directly above the first, is reached by climbing the ramp (fourth class) to the right of the bottom cave. Scramble through a bush to the second cave and traverse left for 20 feet to a rock horn above bushes. Rope up and face climb up and to the right of the horn. Proceed directly up to a narrow ledge which is followed out to the right. Protection here is poor. Approximately 20 feet right of a pocket, head up above a ledge into the third cave. From the third cave traverse left and up, around a large block. Easy climbing leads up a ramp to the right into the fourth and last cave. Traverse right about 20 feet. Climb up past a bulge by way of a small manzanita bush in a crack. Above this, follow easy cracks and slabs to the summit. FA Herbert Rickert et al., 1959.

170
Long Gone Bong
★ **5.6**

This is the right-facing corner just left of the start of the *South Face* route. Straight forward climbing leads to a dirty crack where a diagonal traverse may be made back to the left. Continue this traverse along a ceiling and around a corner to the tiny belay ledge mentioned at the top of the first pitch on the *South Face* route. Finish via the top two pitches of the *South Face* route. FA Amos Clifford and Joe Roland, 1974.

171
South Face
★ ★ **5.7**

At a point about fifty feet to the east (right) of the bottom cave, there is a prominent left-facing, left-leaning crack. Lieback directly up this crack until it peters out. Climb a short section of face to a tiny belay ledge about 70 feet off the ground. The next pitch goes up a right-facing corner and over the face above the top of the corner. Continue to the last cave and final section of the *Cave Route*.
FA Mike Forkash and Gary Anderson, late 1970's.

171a. 5.8 Below the belay ledge mentioned at the top of the first pitch, traverse up and right to an edge. Above this, head up and then back left to a corner. Once again climb back out onto the face to the right. Face moves lead to an overhanging, right-leaning corner. Follow this ceiling until it is possible to climb over it and join back up with the regular route.
FA Mike Forkash and Gary Anderson, late 1970's.

172
Dream Weaver
5.10+ (R)

To the right of the *South Face* route climb the smooth, poorly protected face, rejoining the upper section of the *Cave Route*. FA Mike Forkash and friend, late 1970's.

173
Southeast Chute
5.4

This route follows the main chute at the eastern edge of the main face. Scramble up and left to a small ledge with loose rock and small plants atop it. Climb the rotten rock above. Enter and follow the chute which opens out to the right of a large block and bush. Continue up and left on easier ground to the summit. FA Chrys Mitchell and Steve Tucker, mid-1970's.

174
West Face Route
Moderate 5th

Ascend the obvious zig-zag crack system on the West Face. FA Chuck Fitch and Steve Fitch, 1974.

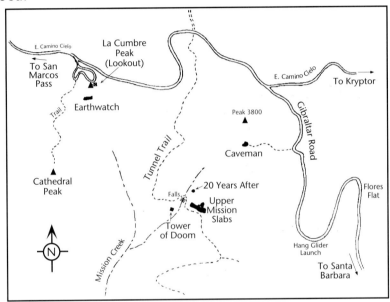

The Caveman

This is the large boulder, with a cave at its base, on the unnamed peak between Gibraltar Rock and La Cumbre Peak. The outcrop sits near the top of the hill among a group of pines facing the ocean. The rock is visible from Gibraltar Rock. The approach starts about 1.2 miles up the road beyond Gibraltar Rock. Start hiking up a small wash on the left, then across the hillside following a faint trail.

175
Caveman
★ 5.11c TR

The route surmounts the right side of the cave/roof and the face above. FTR Pat Holt, Warren Gibbs, and Bob Haas, 1987.

Hermit Rock

Six miles east from the intersection with Gibraltar Road, and about six-tenths of a mile west from Romero Saddle, East Camino Cielo cuts through a formation of solid sandstone. On the north (downhill) slope of this road cut, just below the pavement, sits Hermit Rock. You'll need to keep a sharp lookout for the formation because it is not easily spotted. All you can see from the road is the top of the rock. The formation was named for its hidden location.

The summit is most easily reached by scrambling down the scree slope on the left-hand (west) side of the small ridge leading out from the road. The 130 foot north face of the formation, which faces away from the road, contains several routes. To reach the base of the cliff, scramble down the hillside on the right (east) side of the rock.

Hidden away like it is, Hermit hasn't been climbed as much as other crags closer to town. Care should be taken with lichen and loose holds. Facing north, the climbs are shaded on hotter days. The formation is made up of the oldest sandstone climbed in the tri-county region. The rock is also a bit rougher than most other sandstones with a high content of pebble and cobble inclusions. A small cave at the base of the cliff (no doubt the home of the hermit) provides protection from the elements and falling objects. Take along a selection of pro for all of the routes.

The routes are listed from left to right when facing the cliff.

176
Chunky Monkey
★ 5.11+ TR

Starting at the left-hand side of the north face, climb up steep rock and a seam directly to the obvious roof above. Keep to the left of the rounded cobblestone section. Climb over the center of the roof (crux) with the horizontal pocket under it. Easier climbing leads to the base of a difficult face section. Jog left and climb the arete for only a few feet. Using a round, shallow finger pocket, traverse back to the right onto the steep face . A short, slanting crack at the top of this section marks the end of the difficult climbing. FTR Marc Soltan, December 22, 1991.

177
Tabs
5.6 TR

Starting just left of the cave, head left up an easy ramp to under the first bulge. Ascend a left-leaning slot. Above the slot, diagonal up and right on ledges and face moves until the top section of *Battle of the Bulge* is gained. FTR Gary Tabor, late 1970's.

North Face of Hermit Rock

178
Battle of the Bulge
★★ 5.10+

Starting at the cave, climb straight up, past a bolt, to the obvious bulge about 40 feet off the ground. Several awkward face moves, protected by 3 bolts, lead up over the bulge to a fourth-class trough. Climb a direct line up the trough and over a final overhang to the top. FTR Dick Saum, spring 1979.
FA Kevin Steele and Terry Roland, December 1, 1991.

179
The Recluse
5.7 TR

This route marks the first known climb of the Hermit. The line combines what is now the start of *Battle Of The Bulge* with the horn on the *Wings* route. Finish by pulling over the roof near the top of the central fourth-class trough.
FTR Steve Tucker, mid-1970's.

180
The Wind Beneath
Her Wings
★ 5.8

Starting about 15 feet right of the cave climb the obvious pockets past two bolts to the bulge with a right pointing horn. Pull over the bulge at the horn then head up and right past a fourth bolt. Instead of heading left up the easy trough, traverse right onto the steep, blocky buttress. Make sure you traverse right well below the large abandoned birds nest. Climb up and over a series of bulges past two more bolts to a large ledge with bushes. The last moves head up the short chimney to the top. See photo on page iii.
FTR Libby Whaley, December 22, 1991.
FA Libby Whaley and Judy Patton, February 2, 1992.
The route is dedicated to Libby's father.

Marc Soltan on an early attempt of Chunky Monkey. *Photo: Steve Tucker*

Kevin Steele leading
Battle of the Bulge.
Photo: Steve Tucker

181
The Axis
5.7

Some thirty feet right and uphill from the small cave at the base of the north face, climb easy blocks and ledges for about 20 or 30 feet. When possible, traverse left to link up with the fourth-class trough of the upper north face.
FA Don and Kelley Long, October 1985.

182
The Excuse
Easy 5th TR

The route has the same beginning as *The Axis*. Instead of traversing left to *The Recluse*, diagonal up and right to sloping ledges and follow a dirty dihedral. Finish with the chimney at the top of the *Wings* route. FTR Amos Clifford, mid-1970's.

The Kryptor

The Chumash indians considered quartz crystal to be a powerful talisman. They connected it with rain, thunder, and lightning. It was believed that the houses of the "higher beings" were made of quartz crystal.

One mile east of Hermit Rock lies a unique formation of hard Blueschiste. This is the site of Santa Barbara's first "sport climbing" testpieces. At Romero Saddle, the pavement ends and the dirt road begins. The small crag sits on a ridge downhill toward the Santa Ynez River and can be seen from the road .

Kryptor, also known as Green Dome and Turtle Rock, has two distinct faces developed so far. The west face is clean and overhanging while the opposite east face is friable and shattered. The top of the crag also shares this shattered nature and care should be taken with the abundance of loose rock. For this same reason the majority of routes do not top-out, but instead end at fixed bolt anchors.

Climbers have two choices for approach. The first follows the established Romero Trail for 50 feet to where a climbers trail branches left toward the formation. Alternatively, a more direct path can be taken straight down the ridge from the roadside parking. This follows a recently established trail which is not entirely evident from the road.

The dense and edgy nature of Blueschiste gives the Santa Barbara climber a refreshing change of pace from the usual sandstone.

The routes are described from left to right (as faced from the downhill side), beginning with the east face:

East Face

Best approached from the east side of the formation.

183
This Side of Paradise
★ ★ 5.10c
On the left side of the face. Four bolts to twin-bolt anchor. FA Jeff Buhl, Steve Edwards, and Todd Mei, Spring 1992.

184 **Rock the Kasbar** **5.9**	Climb past four bolts to the double bolt anchor. FTR Jim Tobish, summer 1990.
185 **Hero in a Halfshell** **5.10a TR**	Climb directly past a hole to a two bolt anchor. NOTE: Please stay off this route now that bats have moved into the hole. FTR Dave Griffith, summer 1990.
186 **Piece of the Action** **★ 5.10b**	Start just right of route 185. Six bolts are clipped before the top anchor. FA Steve Edwards and Todd Mei, Spring 1992.
187 **Metamorphosis** **5.9**	Follow four bolts just left of *Piece of the Action*. Care should be taken clipping the third bolt (ground-fall potential). FA Marty Snyder and Dave Griffith, summer 1990.
188 **Anti-Bro** **★ 5.10b**	Start just right of *Metamorphosis*. Four bolts to a double bolt anchor. FA Tony Becchio and Dave Griffith, summer 1990.

189
Dancing Fingers
★★★ 5.10 +

Just right of *Anti-Bro,* follow five bolts to the same anchor. Excellent solid pockets at the start. FA Dave Griffith, summer 1990.

190
Arachnoid Arete
★★ 5.11b

At the far right-hand edge of the east face, climb up under the small roof past a bolt. Follow the arete and face above to a double bolt anchor. Ground-fall potential while clipping the third bolt. FA Dave Griffith and Tony Becchio, summer 1990.

The next route lies about 30 feet right of Arachnoid Arete.

191
For the World is Hollow & I Have Touched the Sky
★ 5.11b

Follow the line of 8 bolts that lead up the entire face. Double bolts at the top. FA Todd Mei and Steve Edwards, Spring 1992.

Pat Briggs Memorial Buttress

This is the large, separated block to the right and uphill from Arachnoid Arete. (As of this printing, Pat Briggs is still alive and kicking!)

192
Looking for Spock's Brain
★ 5.9

Around the corner of the left end of the buttress follow four bolts directly to a double anchor. FA Dave Potter, Todd Mei, and Steve Edwards, Spring 1992.

192a What Have You Done With Spock's Brain? ★5.9+: From the fourth bolt, head right around the corner and up past two more bolts. FA Steve Edwards and Todd Mei, Spring 1992.

193
Patterns of Force
★★ 5.11d

Follow the left edge of the buttress past 6 bolts. FA Steve Edwards and Todd Mei, Spring 1992.

194
Macho Grande
5.12b TR

Starting approximately in the middle of the face, climb directly to a 2-bolt anchor at the top. FTR Sterling Wilson, summer 1990.

*Opposite: Steve Edwards
leading Stealing Fire.
Photo: John Perlin*

195
In the Kingdom of Green Light
5.11a TR

Between *Macho Grande* and the right edge of the face, head up and over the roof to the same anchor bolts.
FTR Pat Briggs, summer 1990.

196
Patriot Roof
5.10a

Climb over the short "roof" on the outcrop between the Pat Briggs Memorial Buttress and *Baby Snakes*.
FTR Steve Edwards, Spring 1993.

West Face

This is the overhanging, west face on the crag. When approached from above, scramble down along the left-hand side of the formation.

197
Baby Snakes
5.9 TR

Short wall that faces the river valley, forming the left side of the West face. FTR Pat Briggs, Tony Becchio, et. al., 1990.

198
That Which Survives
★ 5.11c

Climb the left-hand arete clipping four bolts before reaching the top anchors. FA Dave Talsky, Mark Robinson, and Steve Edwards, Spring 1992.

199
Stealing Fire
★★ 5.12d/13

First attempted (and almost led) by David Griffith in 1990, this route has thwarted many strong attempts . An awkward start on sloping holds leads upward on the far left of the West Face. FA Stuart Ruckman, Spring 1993.

200
Quartz Crystal
★★★ 5.12c/d

Named for the crystal in a niche on the upper section of the route. Starting in the middle of the face, climb fairly directly up past five bolts to the top.
FA Dave Griffith, August 1990.

Dave Griffith leading Quartz Crystal.
Photo: Tim Brown

**Kryptor
West Face**
Photo: Pat Briggs

201 **Dagger of the Mind** ★★ **5.12c**	On the far right of the West Face, four bolts to the anchors. FA Steve Edwards, Spring 1993.

201a: Monsters in the Maze, ★ 5.12a: A link-up from the third bolt on *Quartz Crystal* to the third bolt of *Dagger of the Mind*, finishing on that route. FA Steve Edwards, Spring 1993.

West Camino Cielo

The Brickyard ★ ★ ★

An excellent bouldering area on West Camino Cielo 3.4 miles from the San Marcos Pass Road turnoff.

Hike towards the ocean past an open area full of broken glass and other target practice debris. As the clearing narrows and begins to descend the slope, look for a trail shooting off to the left which diagonals down and left to a group of rocks on the downhill side of the trail. The first boulder in the group can be reached in about five minutes and can be spotted as having a flat top. A wide variety of problems on excellent rock (streaked with stains of red iron) characterize these boulders.

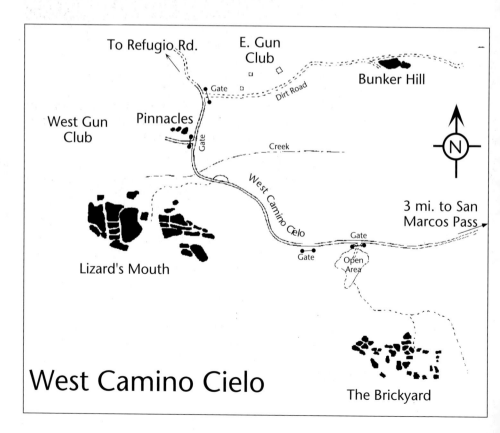

West Camino Cielo

Bouldering at the Brickyard. Photo: Pat Briggs

The Playground ⋆
A boulder field located off West Camino Cielo 2.5 miles from the San Marcos Pass turnoff. An unmarked but well worn trail leads down the hillside towards the ocean.

Lizard's Mouth ⋆ ⋆
Turn west onto Camino Cielo from San Marcos Pass. Park at the last right-hand curve before the gun club (3.7 miles from the San Marcos Pass Road turnoff), and take the unmarked trail that leads off from the left-hand (southwest) side of the road. It is necessary to do a little searching to find solid rock. Since the early 1970's a number of bouldering and top-rope problems have been done in this area, particularly around the Lizard's Mouth Rock itself. Sadly, in 1992 bolt anchors appeared where none had previously been used.

Years ago, this area was pristine, free of broken bottles, graffiti, paper wrappers, gun cartridges, and other signs of man's passing. Today this is not the case. If you would, please help keep this once beautiful spot clean.

Above: Sara Munro on a problem called Meilee *in the Lizards Mouth area. Photo: Steve Edwards*

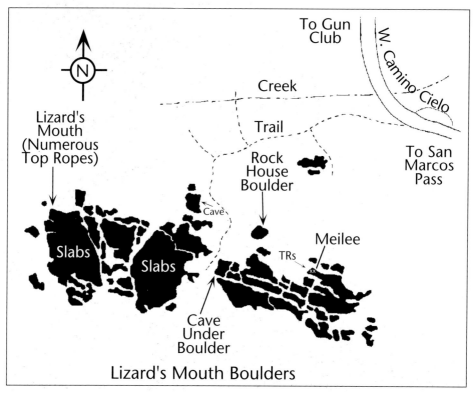

Lizard's Mouth Boulders

Bunker Hill

Located behind (east of) the Winchester Gun Club site and 3.9 miles from the turnoff from San Marcos Pass Road. Access is through the Gun Club when no one is using the shooting range. Although the rocks are within the National Forest it would be wise to contact the Winchester Gun Club management to find out which days the area will not be in use by shooters. There are also a number of good top-rope problems in the area.

202
Saum Route
5.7

Follow the crack up the west prow. The beginning moves are a bit rotten.
FA Dick Saum and Steve Tucker, February 1988.

203
Rock, Salt and Nails
5.9

Climb the obvious crack just left of center on the south wall of the formation. Just past a horizontal seam, the crack heads up and left to the top. FA Libby Whaley and Steve Tucker, 1988.

Santa Ynez River Valley

Gold Chasm

Gold Chasm lies in the Santa Ynez Valley to the north of Santa Barbara. To get there, take Highway 154 over San Marcos Pass to the Paradise Road turnoff. Follow Paradise Road past the first river crossing. Keep to the left and head for the Upper Oso Campground. About one quarter of a mile before the campground itself, the formation can be seen off in the distance to the right. The approach only takes about 15 minutes if you don't follow the creek. Instead, keep high on the left side of the valley.

There are other rock faces in the vicinity of Upper Oso that might provide route possibilities.

204
Schpitzen
★ **5.9/A3**

A short overhanging bolt ladder reaches a crack. Two nut placements give access to sustained jamming. Take a standard rack and small stoppers. An anchor at the top of both this route and *Pot Luck* is established.
FA Gary Anderson and Mike Forkash, pre-1980.

205
Pot Luck
5.8

Climb the potholes to the chimney. Take a couple of large chocks. FA Mike Forkash and Gary Anderson, 1980.

206
Swift Trip
★ ★ **5.11**

A classic lieback (5.8) reaches a ledge where it is possible to lower off or continue diagonally on insecure aid (or 5.11) for the remainder of the crack. FA (5.8/A3) Gary Anderson and Mike Forkash, 1980. FFA Mike Forkash and Matt Clarke, 1980.

The next two routes are hidden further up the canyon's left side to the east of the main wall. The rock is generally of poor quality and dirty. Approach via the creek bed /valley right of the preceding routes.

207
Little Feat
5.7

A wide left-slanting crack on orange rock leads to a dirty chimney.
FA Libby Whaley and Steve Tucker, spring 1989.

208
There You Have It
5.11-

Face leading to a prominent dihedral.
FA Kevin Brown and Kevin Steele, spring 1989.

Gold Chasm

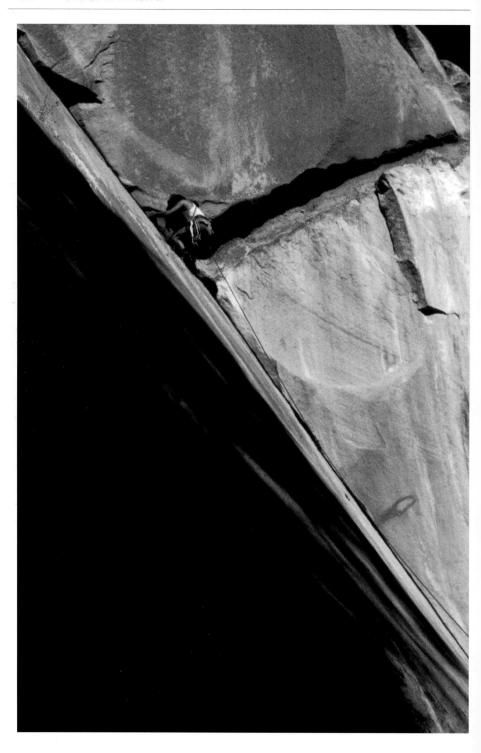

Red Rock

Over San Marcos Pass, at the end of Paradise Road, is Red Rock. The rock, though climbable (and top-roped since the early 1970's) isn't one to recommend. The surrounding creekbed has a few boulders and nice swimming holes. There are also rock slabs of questionable quality upstream from Red Rock.

Gaviota

The cliffs around the Gaviota tunnel, north of Santa Barbara have seen some climbing. Most obvious here is the chimney across the creek from the highway. There seem to be other possibilities in the vicinity. The rock quality is generally rotten.

209
Tunnel Vision
Moderate 5th

This is the most obvious large chimney across the creek as seen from the south entrance to the highway tunnel. *The first ascent was third classed. This was Mike Forkash's first time climbing. Brian Smith recalls Mike's face as being quite white at the time! Mike went on to do the first free lead of Makunaima at Cold Springs Dome.* FA Brian Smith, Doug Hsu, and Mike Forkash, 1975.

210
Flat Iron
5.0-5.7+

This is the large triangular orange slab facing the ocean just west of the rest stop on Highway 101. Many variations are possible. FA David L. Bishop et al., March 1965.

Bald Mountain

There have been several reports of climbable rock on Bald Mountain in the San Rafael Mountains north of Cachuma Lake. The approach is via trails from the Manzana Creek area near Davey Brown campground.

*Opposite:
Swift Trip,
the classic
lieback at
Gold
Chasm.
Photo: Tim
Brown*

Santa Barbara Bouldering

In the years prior to 1980 bouldering wasn't nearly as popular as roped climbing in this area. Since 1980 there has been somewhat of an increase in new boulder problems especially in the vicinity around Santa Barbara. Painted Cave is the best example of this.

Painted Cave ★ ★ ★

Up Painted Cave Road above San Marcos Pass Road, there are several large boulders that overhang and hug the road. They sit about a mile down from the Chumash Painted Cave State Historical Park and contain some of Santa Barbara's finest problems.

Probably the single most prolific person to start things off here was Doug Hsu. Doug, along with Chuck Fitch put up just about all the major problems you find at Painted Cave. Their routes were put up wearing EB's, and sans top-rope or chalk.

More recently, Dave Griffith has been the person pushing the limits. He was the first to climb *Trojan* on the overhanging arete left of Heavy Traffic. Jonny Woodward was the first to boulder the *Hallway Roof* on the east boulder via the obvious seam and line of pockets splitting the length of the ceiling. Woodward was also the first to climb the flake/corner left of *Static Eliminator* (a critical part of the flake has since been broken off).

The bouldering here is right on the road and visible to many non-climbers who drive by. There are also a number of houses within ear shot of the rocks. With this in mind, it would be extremely wise not only to keep the radios turned down, the trash picked up, and park off the road, but also to keep the unsightly use of chalk to a minimum. Some of the land owners and passers-by have thought that the chalk was paint. It would be a shame to lose Santa Barbara's best bouldering spot.

DO NOT climb on the rocks surrounding the Chumash Painted Cave State Historical Park, or the privately-owned boulder field 1/4 mile down the road from the roadside boulders.

Terry Roland on the Cracked Boulder at Painted Cave. Photo: Ivana Noell

Painted Cave

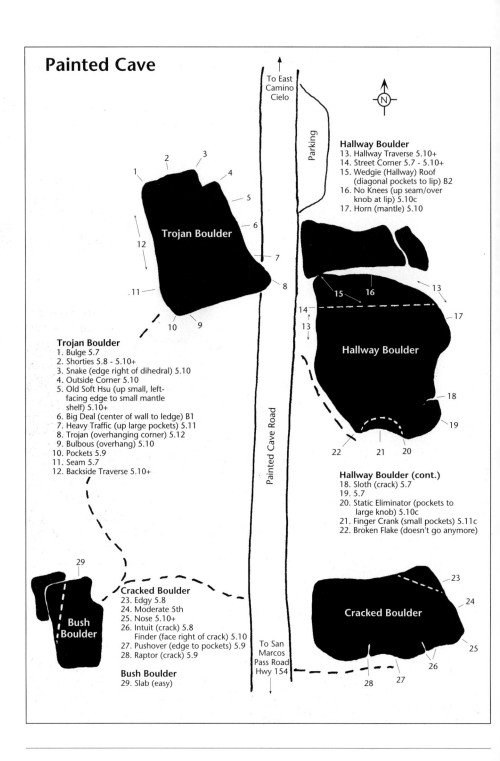

To East Camino Cielo

Parking

N

Trojan Boulder

Painted Cave Road

Hallway Boulder
13. Hallway Traverse 5.10+
14. Street Corner 5.7 - 5.10+
15. Wedgie (Hallway) Roof (diagonal pockets to lip) B2
16. No Knees (up seam/over knob at lip) 5.10c
17. Horn (mantle) 5.10

Hallway Boulder

Trojan Boulder
1. Bulge 5.7
2. Shorties 5.8 - 5.10+
3. Snake (edge right of dihedral) 5.10
4. Outside Corner 5.10
5. Old Soft Hsu (up small, left-facing edge to small mantle shelf) 5.10+
6. Big Deal (center of wall to ledge) B1
7. Heavy Traffic (up large pockets) 5.11
8. Trojan (overhanging corner) 5.12
9. Bulbous (overhang) 5.10
10. Pockets 5.9
11. Seam 5.7
12. Backside Traverse 5.10+

Hallway Boulder (cont.)
18. Sloth (crack) 5.7
19. 5.7
20. Static Eliminator (pockets to large knob) 5.10c
21. Finger Crank (small pockets) 5.11c
22. Broken Flake (doesn't go anymore)

Cracked Boulder
23. Edgy 5.8
24. Moderate 5th
25. Nose 5.10+
26. Intuit (crack) 5.8 Finder (face right of crack) 5.10
27. Pushover (edge to pockets) 5.9
28. Raptor (crack) 5.9

Bush Boulder
29. Slab (easy)

Bush Boulder

Cracked Boulder

To San Marcos Pass Road Hwy 154

West Camino Cielo ★ ★ ★
Excellent bouldering can be found all along West Camino Cielo.

For information on **The Brickyard, The Playground,** and **Lizard's Mouth** see the *West Camino* section on pages 130-132.

Maria Ygnacio Bridge ★ ★
(aka: Patterson Bridge) In Goleta, just south of Patterson Avenue, turn down Lassen off of Hollister Avenue. Park at the intersection of Lassen and San Simeon and walk down the bicycle path to the railroad bridge that crosses Maria Ygnacio Creek. The steep, sandstone bridge abutments make for a great fingertip workout on small edges.

Bouldering at Maria Ygnacio.
Photo: Barry Tessman

Skofield Park ★★

Skofield Park, off of Las Canoas Road, is scattered with a number of smaller boulders offering a variety of difficulties. Any number of questionable climber types could have been key to skulking around these rocks for the first time.

Here again, the use of chalk could cause problems with the park management. As the park ranger changes from time to time, climbers should try and keep a good rapport with those in charge.

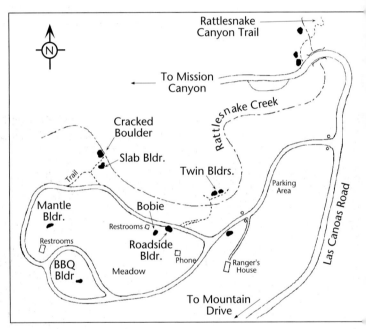

Skofield Park

Westmont College

Westmont College on La Paz Road (off Cold Springs Road) in Montecito offers two boulders of significance.

One rock is directly in front of the Voskyl Library and the other is cloistered between Clark and Page residence halls. This second boulder is well hidden in a grove of small trees and scrub, recognizable by the single palm tree which shades the boulder's summit. Both rocks offer short, overhanging face moves.

Santa Barbara Miscellanea

UCSB Indoor Climbing Wall

In April of 1991 the Adventure Programs Department of UCSB opened an artificial sport climbing wall in Robertson Gym. The indoor climbing area contains a bouldering wall about 11 feet high and 40 feet long as well as several 20 foot high top-rope routes. The structure was designed by Jade Chun and Steve Tucker. The facility is open to the public. Check with the Adventure Programs office at the university for operating hours and fees.

Virgin rock in Santa Barbara's backcountry. Photo: Steve Tucker

Ventura

The climbs of Ventura County are not only widely spread apart, they are also diverse in geologic origin. Most of Ventura's climbs have been done on sandstone. These outcrops extend from Mugu Rock on the southern coastline to larger exposures in the Ojai Valley and Sespe Gorge.

The southern reaches of the county touch upon the volcanic rock of the Santa Monica Mountains. The majority of these pocketed faces have yet to be explored for their climbing potential. An example of the quality of the rock can be found at the boulder in Camarillo Grove Park.

Foothill Crag, sometimes known as "The Foot," is located just outside of Ojai at the very north end of Foothill Road. Other than the Sespe Gorge area, Foothill Crag contains the highest density of routes for any single crag in Ventura County.

Shaded in the afternoon, it is an ideal spot for hot summer days. It is also remote enough to escape the sounds of downtown Ojai.

Foothill Crag

From Ojai Avenue (Highway 150) in downtown Ojai, turn onto North Signal St. at the only stoplight in town. Continue past a jog at Grand Avenue. Turn left (across from 203 N. Signal) at the Los Padres National Forest sign that reads "Pratt/Foothill Trailhead." Drive past the large water tank and continue into the trailhead parking area. The trail begins at the lower end of the parking area and heads uphill along Stewart Creek (see map on page 152).

A twenty-five minute walk leads to the crag. The trail crosses two dirt roads, passes through an old Eucalyptus grove and eventually connects with the upper section of Foothill Road. The trail utilizes a public right-of-way. All the land surrounding the approach trail is privately owned.

Continue up Foothill Road until a trail branches off to the right. This leads to the base of the crag.

The rock is a gritty sandstone with a few cracks and many high quality face climbs protected for the most part with bolts. There are several easy ways to scramble or walk off the top of the formation.

Good bouldering can be found just to the east up the trail paralleling the main cliff face.

Probably the earliest people to climb on the "Foot" were Yvon Chouinard and Tex Bossier back in the 1960's. The crag saw little activity until Reese Martin showed up in the 1980's. Making first ascents in the traditional style (from the ground up), Martin almost single-handedly opened up the formation's face climbing potential.

Foothill Crag

211
K-Mart Kidnap
5.8 (R)

Climb up via an undercling and reach for the very large (7 foot diameter) hueco. Climb up and over the top of the hueco to the ledge above. The route ends here.
FA Reese Martin (solo), February 1986.

212
Bijou
★ ★ **5.9+**

Face climb up the overlaps and scoop, past two bolts to a ledge. Going left at the second bolt is harder (5.10+). From the ledge, face climb past a small roof to a steep headwall with two bolts.
FA Reese Martin and Bill Powers, May 1986.

212a. Upper Headwall Variation (rating unknown).
FA unknown, 1990.

213
In a Rut
5.8 (R)

Face climb to the ledge. It's possible to clip the first bolt on *Bijou* or tie-off the metal posts.
FA Reese Martin (solo), March 1986.

214
Pioneer Direct
5.8

Lieback the left-facing flake/corner below the "Pioneer Posts" (metal rods) then climb up to the cave. Protection can be had by tying off these posts.
FA Reese Martin (solo), 1986.

215
Big Bolts
5.0

Start by heading up the obvious ramp to the right then traversing left across easy moves past the metal posts to the cave.
FA unknown.

The following routes start from the obvious cave partway up the left side of the wall:

216
ummin' for Splatter
★ ★ ★ **5.11b**

Begin as for *Big Bolts* but climb directly up the slab past a bolt to the cave. Head straight up and over the cave past two bolts to a roof. Turning the roof is the crux. Easier climbing on the headwall above leads to the top. An assortment of cams is recommended.
FA Steve Mrazek and Reese Martin, September 1987.

217
Original Route
5.7

From the cave climb up and right to the obvious corner above. Staying below the corner follow it up and left to the top. Finding pro can be tricky.
FA Tex Bossier and friend, 1960's.

218
I Love L.A.
★ ★ ★ 5.9 (R)

From the cave climb up the shallow corner past a bolt to the roof. Move right and mantel over the roof. Above the roof is a fixed Lost Arrow piton. Easier climbing leads to the top.
FA Bill Powers, Mark Sargent, and Reese Martin, February 1986.

Reese Martin encountering
Ruthless Poodles.
Photo: Kevin Steele

The following routes start on the ground just right of the large cave:

219
Ruthless Poodles
★ ★ ★ 5.10a

From directly below a three foot diameter hueco (at the same height as the cave), climb the slab to the hueco. Tricky moves protected by bolts lead up the headwall to the top. An excellent route. FA Reese Martin (roped solo), 1986.

220
The Crack
5.6

The obvious crack splitting the left-hand face.
FA Yvon Chouinard et. al., early 1970's.

221
Clean Sweep
★ ★ 5.9

Thin face climbing to the right of *The Crack* leads to a bolt. Easier climbing leads to a final roof protected by a bolt. Bring small nuts. FA Tim Coates and Mike Moore, January 1987.

222
Sob Story
5.8

A series of mantels gain a bolt. Climb up and past a flake to a second bolt which protects the steep finish. Bring a selection of cams. FA Reese Martin and Dale Buckstaff, March 1987.

The following routes are on the main face to the right of the central gully:

223
Blown Out
5.9

From under the left end of the roof with a bolt, layback left and mantel up. Climb the crack above to the top. Bring a selection of nuts. FA unknown, late 1986.

224
Overblown
5.8

From under the roof, hand traverse up and right past a fixed pin to the same finish as *Blown Out*. FA Reese Martin and Steve Offerman, December 1986.

224a. Instead of hand traversing right, pull straight over the roof at the bolt. FA unknown, 1988.

225
Moon Doggies
★ ★ 5.8

Starting under the roof, climb out the diagonalling crack and onto the face above. A fixed pin (added later) protects the next move up the crack which contains several fine moves before reaching good holds. Other than the fixed pin, clean protection can be used on the entire route. FA Reese Martin (solo), February 1986.

226
Teetering
★ ★ 5.10d TR

Climb the short slab right of *Moon Doggies* past two bolts to a seam. A thin layback here is the crux. Hangers may be missing. FTR Reese Martin and Bill Powers, December 1986. FA Steve Mrazek, September 1987.

227
From the Ashes
5.10b ★ ★ ★

From a large pocket and the first bolt, small edges lead to a second bolt. Climb the small right-facing corner to the top. FA Reese Martin (roped solo), January 1987.

Reese almost lost his head on this one...(his self-belay caught him head-first—inches off the ground).

228
Water Groove
5.8 (R)

The obvious water chute on the right side of the wall. FA Reese Martin (solo), January 1987.

Bouldering at Foothill

A couple of problems (5.8/5.9) lie on the 20 foot boulder above *Water Groove*.

Reese Martin, rising From the Ashes.
Photo: Kevin Steele

Shelf Ridge

Shelf Ridge is the first rocky ridge on the north side of the Ojai valley. It is approached via a fifteen minute walk up the trail near the end of Gridley Road. Routes are 20-60 feet in height. (See map on the next page.)

Drive east on Ojai Avenue. (Highway 150) past the main part of town. Turn north up Gridley Road. Park at the end. The Foothill trailhead sign will be seen just to the left before you park. About 100 yards below the Foothill trailhead sign an asphalt road heads off into a grove. Head up the paved road (which is a Forest Service trail easement) to just past an old water tank. At the first right-hand turn, veer left across the small creek onto the poorly maintained Foothill Trail. Follow the Foothill Trail along the hillside until it gains the ridge.

229
Homoneering
5.11b

The crux is exceedingly thin face climbing on the last 30 feet. Two bolts at midway, close together on rock with tortoise shell texture. FA Reese Martin and Steve Doty, January 1987.

230
Horseman Clutch
5.10c

Thin face climbing up a wiggly seam left of *Homoneering*. FA Reese Martin and Steve Doty, January 1987.

231
Fortune and Glory
5.11a TR

Climb the right side of the slab *Homoneering* is on. FTR Reese Martin and Steve Doty, January 1987.

232
Flakey
5.9

Steep face climbing on flakes on the east side of the third tower east of the saddle where the trail from Gridley Road meets the ridge. FA Reese Martin (solo), April 1986.

233
Christmas Present
5.9

This is the 40 foot high, left leaning finger and hand crack facing the Ojai valley 100 yards east of the saddle where the trail meets the ridge. FA Reese Martin (solo), Christmas day 1987.

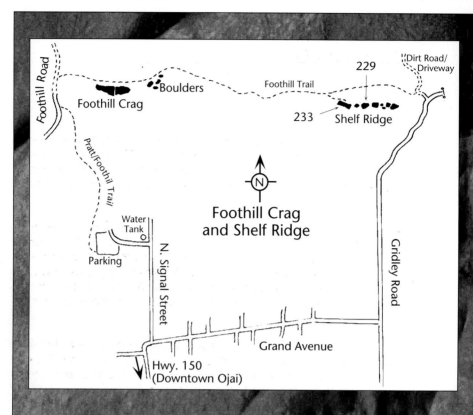

Dirt Road/Driveway

229

Foothill Trail

Boulders

233   Shelf Ridge

Foothill Road

Foothill Crag

Pratt/Foothill Trail

Water Tank

N

Foothill Crag and Shelf Ridge

Parking

N. Signal Street

Gridley Road

Grand Avenue

Hwy. 150 (Downtown Ojai)

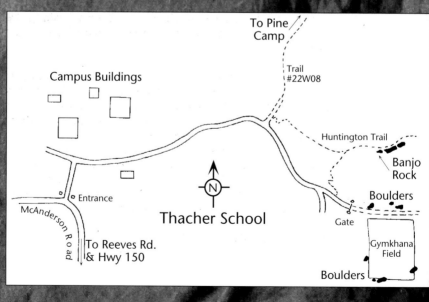

To Pine Camp

Campus Buildings

Trail #22W08

Huntington Trail

Banjo Rock

Boulders

N

Entrance

McAnderson Road

Thacher School

Gate

Gymkhana Field

To Reeves Rd. & Hwy 150

Boulders

Thacher School Rocks

The Thacher School area has excellent bouldering and top-roping in an idyllic, private setting. The climbing is on Thacher School property and, while climbers are welcome, the owners request that you refrain from using chalk or placing fixed protection.

Drive east on Ojai Avenue. (Highway 150) out of downtown Ojai. Turn left onto Reeves Road then left onto McAnderson Road. Continue on McAnderson Road until you see the entry to Thacher School on the right. Bear to the right when driving into the school and follow the signs towards Gymkhana and Jameson Field. Drive slowly to avoid dust problems and respect all gates.

About 20 boulders are scattered about Jameson Field. Try starting at the Jameson plaque boulder at Gymkhana field. There are also some good problems on the pointed boulder at the far side of the field (look out for poison oak).

The ravine on the backside of the low ridge directly north of Jameson field has some excellent face and crack climbs. Laying in a cool, shaded ravine this is a good place for hot summer days.

To get there, drive on the road past Jameson field and past the trailhead (#22W08) to Pine Camp. A couple of turns beyond the trailhead will bring you to a fork in the road, the left of which is distinguished by two white metal posts on either side. It is best to park at the dirt area in front of the Pine Camp trailhead. Walk back past the white metal posts to the first trail leading off to the left (Huntington Trail). Keep to the right on the trail which follows a small creek bed. Not too far up the trail you'll see the short, 30 to 40 foot high rock faces on the right. The rock is generally of good quality with steep face moves on small edges and nubbins. The lower of the two main faces is called "Banjo Rock".

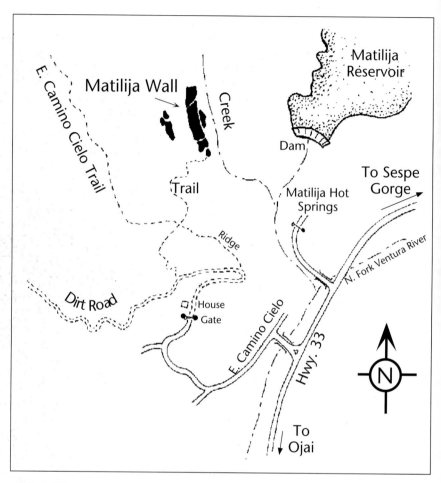

Matilija Wall

While driving to Sespe Gorge on Highway 33, you'll pass by the Matilija Hot Springs. From the highway a large cliff face can be seen high up in a small valley above the hot springs.

The unusual thing about this particular crag is that it is the single largest sandstone cliff in the tri-counties. It reaches a height of over 350 feet and a length of approximately 1000 feet. The formation is of the same Matilija Sandstone that Gibraltar Rock is made of. What is even more unusual about this formation is that it sat virtually untouched for 20 years after seeing its first route established. It wasn't until early 1993 that Dana Hollister began to explore the cliff for its full potential.

As of this writing all of the routes on the crag have been put up on lead (from the ground up) and with bolts used very sparingly. Local Ojai climbers have voiced their desire that future climbing parties respect the traditional standard of establishing routes that has been preserved in this area.

To reach the cliff, turn off of Highway 33 onto Camino Cielo just before the Matilija Hot Springs turnoff. Camino Cielo winds up the hillside and seems to disappear into someone's driveway. This is the National Forest access into the hills above.

The road actually goes right through a private yard complete with no trespassing signs. Past this point the road snakes its way up the hillside above, often splitting off into different forks and sub-trails. You'll need to keep taking forks that lead up the center of the main slope above the private property. About halfway up the this large hillside, and well hidden in the brush, is a trail shooting off to the right around the main ridge (in the direction of the dam). This trail is a key element to the approach. It can also be found by simply hiking up the main ridge just west of the private property (which also affords a fairly frequent view of the dam and lake below).

Continue along this trail, contouring towards the cliff, until you reach a large saddle. From the saddle, traverse around to the right directly across a steep hillside. If you're lucky, you'll be able to follow a faint path winding it's way across this section. Once across the steep hillside you'll want to drop down a ridge a short distance, then cut left along the top of the steep drop-off. You'll now be heading straight for the upper east end of the formation.

The base of the north face can be reached by way of gullies, scrambling, down-climbing and/or rappelling. It's a new area and has a lot of loose rock and poison oak waiting for the unsuspecting explorer, so be careful.

**Dick Saum on first pitch of the *Chouinard-Bossier*
Photo: Steve Tucker.**

East Face—Matilija Wall
(aka End O' Wall)

---

234 At the far left of the wall, start just right of the tree. A single
Solitaire bolt protects face moves leading to flakes above. Slightly
5.10- (R) runout. FA Dana Hollister (solo) April 18, 1993.

*As of this writing there is an unfinished route leading up the obvious
ramp/seam in the middle of the face. A bolt placed partway up
marks the current high point.*

---

235 Ascend the obvious chimney. Rotten in places with chock-
Pelvic Thruster stones that should be treated with care.
5.5 FA John Howard and Dana Hollister, April 7, 1993.

North Face—Matilija Wall

The base of the north face can be reached via two routes:

To access the area around the *Chouinard-Bossier* route scramble down the steep hillside directly below *Pelvic Thruster*. A short rappel from a tree leads to ledges and ramps leading down to the bottom of the main cliff face.

The routes on the middle and righthand (west) side of the main wall are best reached by scrambling down ramps and ledges to the double bolts at the top of the *Poison* route. Rappel from the bolts to *Knots Landing* ledge, a large vegetated ramp traversing a good portion of the face.

236
Chouinard-Bossier
★ ★ ★ **5.9**

Ascends the most obvious cracks and dihedrals on the left side of the main north wall. An old piton protects the hand traverse up and right of the first blocky ledge.
FA Yvon Chouinard and Tex Bossier, late 1970's.

237
Black Jack
5.10b

From partway up *Knot's Landing* ledge, start at the base of the distinctive right-facing flake. From a large tree, mantle onto a small ledge and traverse left into the flake. The crux is passing the first chockstones. Continue up the flake and then exit along the left-leaning ramp.
FA Dana Hollister and Brian Crowder, April 3, 1993.

238
Poison
5.7

From the middle of *Knot's Landing* climb the squeeze chimney. A bolt protects the crux moves past a chockstone near the center of the route. Belay at the top of the chimney. 5.4 moves on the face to the right lead to double bolts above. FA John Howard, Dana Hollister and Brian Crowder, March 6, 1993.

239
Crazy Horse
5.7

From the first bolt on *Poison*, traverse right onto the face. Move up and right to a belay above a flake. Continue up the face to where it joins with a crack. 5.7 moves lead to the top.
FA Brian Crowder and Dana Hollister, April 3, 1993.

240
Abortion
5.5

This route actually leads up to *Knot's Landing* itself. It ascends the short wall via left leaning ramps just below *Poison*.
FA Dana Hollister and Mike Mesko, March 20, 1993.

North Face of Matilija Wall

241
Holey Face
5.10a
Further right along *Knot's Landing,* climb the moderate fifth class face full of holes and flakes. Protection can be placed in the holes. Move up and right to a bolt protecting the crux move. Up and right again are double rappel bolts. FA Dana Hollister and Mike Mesko, March 20, 1993.

242
Retreat Route
5.5
Right of *Holey Face,* the moves are predominantly easy fifth class with knobs and horns that can be slung for protection. Climb up and left along the ramps. An awkward move leads to the ledge with the double rap bolts. FA Brian Crowder, John Howard and Dana Hollister, March 6, 1993.

243
Fear Factor
5.9+
Follow a series of finger cracks leading up from the rap bolts mentioned above. Traverse right along a horizontal crack to a bushy belay ledge. Third class to the top. FA John Howard, Brian Crowder and Dana Hollister, March 6, 1993.

244
Reset
5.10/A3
From the rap bolts, turn the corner to the right and follow the flake up and right. At the top of the flake, move out the overhang (A3 seam) and mantle onto a belay ledge. Tied off Lost Arrows and Knifeblades were used on the FA. FA Dana Hollister and John Howard, April 7, 1993.

245
Wet Dream
5.5
On the far right side of *Knot's Landing,* climb the bushy ledge that leads up and left. A 5.5 hand traverse continues along the same ledge up and left. FA Dana Hollister and John Howard, spring 1993.

246
The Gecko
5.8
Begins at the end of the hand traverse on *Wet Dream.* Water streaks (2 bolts) lead straight up to a large right-facing dihedral that leads to the top. FA Brain Crowder, John Howard, and Dana Hollister, April 1993.

247
Pancake Flake
5.5
From the bushy ledge area at the beginning of *Wet Dream* (further down the ramp from the start of *The Gecko*), moderate fifth class moves lead up and right to a ledge with a tree. Head left from the ledge to join the right side of the "pancake" flake and continue up to the top. FA John Howard, Brain Crowder, and Dana Hollister, April 1993.

248
Flying Longhair
5.10

From the ledge right of the "pancake" (top of *Woodstock* second pitch), climb up and right through the overhang (protected by a bolt) to the face above. Continue up a flake (5.8) to face moves past a second bolt. FA Brian Crowder, Dana Hollister, and John Howard, spring 1993.

249
Woodstock
5.10b/A2

Beyond the right end of *Knot's Landing* ledge is a very obvious left leaning ramp. Start at the bottom and two full pitches will take you to the top. Be cautious of dangerous flakes on the first pitch. Beyond these flakes is a good belay ledge. The crux moves are on the second pitch, just before reaching the ledge where *Flying Longhair* crosses through. Double rap bolts will be found a little further along the *Woodstock* ramp.
FA Dana Hollister et al, spring 1993.

Opposite: Mike Mesko
following Holey Face.
Photo: Dana Hollister

Photo: Yvon Chouinard

Sespe Gorge

Heading north out of the city of Ventura, Highway 33 leads through the Ojai valley then winds its way over and through the Santa Ynez and Pine mountains. Out of Ojai, the road closely follows the Matilija Creek drainage until it crests Dry Lakes Ridge just past the Rose Valley turnoff. From here it drops down into and follows the Sespe River valley upstream through Sespe Gorge. The Gorge contains some of the longest technical rock routes in the tri-counties.

Sespe Gorge is about 58 miles from Santa Barbara and about 33 miles out of Ventura.

It is interesting to note that during hard cold snaps in the wintertime, it is possible to see ice smears coming off the cliffs at Black Wall, and the Potrero John slabs! Call ahead for road closure info during stormy weather.

The obvious blocky formation that lies across the creek to the left (north) just before reaching the Gorge itself has been climbed on. No defined routes have been recorded, nor have any sterling accounts of quality climbing cropped up.

The Friends store just out of Ojai on the drive up Highway 33 is a great place to pick up munchies. The Pine Mountain Inn north of the Gorge provides a relaxing spot for shade and drink on hot summer days.

Sometimes referred to as "Black Wall," the main wall at Sespe Gorge reaches a height of approximately 300 feet, becoming more broken and brush covered near the top.

The majority of the routes on this face follow the various crack systems which begin in the creek bed at the base of the wall. For the most part, protection is good and all of the routes mentioned can be led with chocks. Much of the climbing consists of face moves next to cracks, using the cracks for protection.

One should be aware of loose rock even on the more popular lines. Lichen can also be a problem.

A walk-off descent route can be found on the backside of the cliff. There are also fourth class descent routes down the gullies in the center of the wall.

Other than Mugu Rock, Sespe was the scene of Ventura's first roped climbs, and probably the county's first climbs established on lead. Many of the routes listed as having unknown first ascents were no doubt first climbed by early pioneers such as Yvon Chouinard, Dick Blankenbecler or William Thompson during the mid-1960's and early 1970's.

250
Floyd
5.7

On the far left-hand side of the main wall, undercling a right-leaning overhang. Easier climbing for about 20 feet leads to a broken, bushy ledge. From the ledge, traverse right then wander up through a series of corners and blocks to a section of easy face holds to the top. FA unknown.

251
Half Ascent
5.5

In the middle of the face between *Floyd* and the cable platform sits a blocky overhang with a bushy tree atop it. From directly below this formation, climb as directly as possible to its left side. Continue up the left-hand side of the slab to a tree. Either rappel from the tree or continue to the top of the formation via easier climbing. FA Chip Carron and friend, fall 1967.

252
McTavish
★★5.6

From the point where *Half Ascent* gains the lower left-hand edge of the large slab, use edges and ledges to zig-zag a course for a right-leaning ceiling some 40 feet up and left. Climb over a flake in the ceiling to a section of easy, but unprotected slab climbing. FA Yvon Chouinard and Bob McTavish, mid-1970's.

This was the first and probably the last climb for the world-class surfing champion for which the climb is named.

252a. 5.7 Once at the right-leaning ceiling on the route, proceed up and right along the book. A mantel (5.7) is the crux to reaching easier ground. FA unknown.

253
Hangin' Round
5.5

Right of the beginning of the *McTavish* route, a left-leaning seam leads up to the left side of the first blocky roof described in the *McTavish* route. Traverse out to the right under the roof, until it is possible to pull up and over to easy climbing. FA Chrys Mitchell and friend, mid-1970's.

254
Chip's Block
5.6

As directly as possible, climb up to the right of the roof mentioned in the description for the *Hangin' Round* route. Follow the long ceiling up and to the right, then continue up into the brush and broken blocks above. FA unknown, mid-1960's.

255
Slime Climb
5.3

Climb the prominent crack just down stream from the large alcove by the pipe tower. There are a few bushes that can be used for protection points. The second pitch is mostly fourth class to the top of the formation.
FA William Thompson and J. Bryant, February 26, 1967.

The first ascent was made shortly after a rain storm, thus giving the lichen covered rock a very "slimey" surface.

256
The Wasp
★ 5.8

From under the alcove behind the cable platform, climb the crack and flake on the left side of the alcove. Easier crack and face moves lead up to a small tree near the top of the wall and right of a ceiling. Traverse left and pass through the ceiling by one of the following variations: FA unknown, 1970's.

256a. The first notch (5.7) up and left of the small tree.

256b. A left-leaning crack (5.8) several feet to the left of the first variation.

256c. Further yet to the left, another left-leaning crack splits the roof (5.9) and heads into the bushes above.

257
The Sting
★ ★ 5.10+

At the top, center of the alcove mentioned in *The Wasp*, use face holds to reach jams (strenuous) leading over the ceiling. Once above the roof, continue on easier face moves up and to the right to a crack leading directly for the small tree and variations mentioned at the end of *The Wasp*.
FA unknown, 1970's.

258
Mrs. Murphy's
Rusty Old Packard
5.5

Some 20 or 30 feet to the right of the steel platform , and in the center of an area of weathered niches in the cliff, ascend a seam and crack up and left into the fourth class gully.
FA Dick Blankenbecler et al., pre-1975.

David Abeloe at the roof of The Sting.
Photo: Bob Simmons

259
Pipe Prime
5.6
Climb the crack and seam system between *Mrs. Murphy's* and *Pipe Cleaner* as directly as possible, passing over two holes in the wall, to the fourth class gully.
FA John Botke and R. Blankenbecler, March 15,1968.

260
Pipe Cleaner
★ 5.6
Some 40 or 50 feet to the right of the cable platform a pipe is attached to the wall. Climb the crack that starts at the pipe and head directly to the fourth class gully above.
FA unknown, mid-1960's.

261
White Spider
★ 5.6
Between *Pipe Cleaner* and the *Ending Crack*, a thin crack leads straight up past a light colored spot on the face. Continue to the fourth class gully above the dead pine. A few wired stoppers would be good to have along. FA unknown, pre-1965.

262
Ending Crack
★ ★ ★5.7
(aka: Grass to Grass) This route is the obvious straight crack in the middle of the face. Near its top, the crack peters out, and face moves lead directly up to complete the route. Another way to finish the route (and the most popular) is to traverse right and up just below the point where the crack ends (5.6), to the top of *Tree Root*.
FA Don Lauria and Dennis Henneck or Tom Ridenour, 1960's.

263
Tree Root
★ ★ ★5.5
(aka: Long Climb Direct) To the left of a large pine tree and bushy, broken slab, a seam and/or face moves lead up to a crack system and a series of small pine trees. Beyond the first tree, the crack heads up and left. It is wise to do the section beyond the first tree in two short pitches, although it can be done with a single 165 foot rope. This route is an excellent multi-pitch beginners route. FA Herbert Rickert et al., 1959 (via first pitch of Long Climb).

By all accounts, this route was the first to be climbed in the Gorge. Since a direct start was more difficult, the original ascent traversed to the first pine tree using the beginning part of the "Long Climb".

263a (moderate fifth class): Traverse out to the right before topping out in the fourth class gully. Head right a few feet, then up through blocks and ledges.

264
The Boss Man
Difficult 5th
Just up the gully above the top of *Tree Root,* climb a hand crack splitting an overhang on the right side of the same gully.
FA Tex Bossier, mid-1970's.

265
Wadka
5.7

Ascend the face between the first pitch of *Tree Root* and *Ending Crack*. Join up with *Ending Crack* about halfway up the second pitch of that route. FA Yvon Chouinard, 1980.

266
Long Climb
5.6

Starting from the large pine tree up and to the right of the beginning of *Tree Root*, climb up and left to the first tree on *Tree Root*. Rather than heading up the the crack system that diagonals up and left, head straight up a full pitch until just below a small tree. Diagonal up and right into a blocky area. Wander to the top. FA unknown, pre-1965.

267
Crispy Corn Flakes
5.5

Climb the first pitch of *Tree Root*. Belay at the tree and climb up to a large hole. Traverse right from the hole and head up and right (poorly protected) to a niche. Head up and left over flakes past two cracks leading into the bushes.
FA Chrys Mitchell and Steve Tucker, 1972.

268
Pine to Pine
★ 5.6

Starting from the large pine tree at the left-hand side of the bushy, broken slab, head directly up a crack-seam. The route leads towards another good sized pine at the top of the wall. A few small stoppers are good to have along. FA unknown.

269
Hairy Airy
5.7

This route begins up and to the right of the *Pine to Pine* route. Head for a bush part way up the wall. Continue past the bush following seams and face holds as directly as possible to the top. This is not a very popular route.
FA W. Thompson and G. Nelson, pre-1970.

270
Brush-up
5.6

Starting just uphill from *Hairy Airy,* this route is very similar to that route, loose and dirty.
FA unknown.

271
Leaning Tower
5.5

A loose climb that leads up the left-hand side of the large broken slab that lies between the two most prominent gullies on the face. FA R. Blankenbecler and G. Nelson, February 19, 1967.

Descent for the following routes is by way of the fourth class gully on the right-hand edge of the wall. The top of the gully can be most easily negotiated by using a cave behind a large block. Care should be taken with loose rock while in the gully.

272
Top-O-De-Slab
5.6

From the top of the broken slab mentioned in the preceding routes, follow a crack past small bushes to face moves and the top. FA unknown.

273
Bee Line
★ 5.7

On the right side of the large broken slab, follow a thin crack up to a small tree growing 10 or 15 feet out from the slab. The route leads directly up the seam and crack to the top. Very near the top, a block and small shrub sometimes conceal a bees nest. Other than the possibility of angry bees, the route is rather enjoyable. FA Steve Tucker and Joe Roland, late 1970's.

274
Edge of Night
★ ★ 5.7

The outer left-hand edge of the right-hand gully forms this route. Face holds lead up the edge which has a few poorly protected sections. FA unknown, as early as 1976.

Joe Roland on
Tree Root
Photo: Steve Tucker

275
Final Solution
5.7
From halfway up the left-hand side of the gully mentioned in the *Edge of Night* description, climb the left-hand wall. FA unknown, probably Tex Bossier, pre-1980.

276
Half-Nelson
5.2
Starts around the corner from the main wall that lies right of the main right-hand fourth class gully. Proceed up on the main face and the arete. At the top of the pitch is a short wall which can be surmounted by using the crack on the left or the face itself. A suitable climb for beginners. FA unknown.

An early ascent party of the route found an old manila rope rappel anchor on the arete.

277
Rottenrete
5.4
This route lies to the right of *Half-Nelson*. It is the first large arete past, but also overlooking, the major portion of the wall. The route follows the arete and then traverses right on a shelf to a lay-back which leads back to the arete proper. Continue up the arete to a belay at the base of an open book chimney. The second pitch ascends the chimney, eases off and ends at a brushy wide area which can be crossed un-roped (starting to sound like quite the adventure!) until the edge of the main face is gained. A variation of the second pitch is to move left out of the open book under a clean brown overhang just above a small tree. The overhang is easily surmounted and leads up the arete to the brush). The third pitch heads left and up across the main face to a cave beneath the wall's topmost point. Pass through the cave to an overlook of a large chimney. Rappel via large trees.
FA R. Blankenbecler and W. Thompson, February 12, 1967.

Almost directly across the road from the Final Solution *route on the main wall, several cracks next to the road have been climbed as well as a steep, bolted face route.*

278
Roadside Cracks
★ 5.10+
There are three cracks on the left end of the wall; the furthest left is overhanging and very thin. Hand holds on the face have been used to ascend the crack which goes at a hard 5.10. The two cracks immediately to the right of the thin crack are more moderate fifth class routes. All of these lines have been climbed since the beginning of time. FA unknown.

Kevin Brown climbing Glory Days.
Roadside Cracks *are visible.*
Photo: Dr. Lori Brown

279
Glory Days
★ 5.11c

Across the road from the main Sespe Wall lies a strenuous 40 foot high face with two holes. Above the second hole is the first of four bolts. High quality face climbing leads to a two bolt belay/rappel anchor at the top.
Kevin Brown, Menzo Baird, 1985.

Across the road from the cable platform are a few good boulder problems with mantels being the order of the day.

Potrero John

About one-half mile up the road from Sespe's main wall is a section of rock slabs on the left-hand (south) side of the road. These slabs are of similar rock quality as that of the main wall. There are two separate areas across the creek from the road.

Potrero John Wall

On the left, and starting from the sandy creek bed, is a blank-looking face (Potrero John Wall) with a lesser slab on its right side. A tree stands in front of the lesser slab. The "Potrero Wall" is about 60 to 80 feet in height. The lesser slab, called the Practice Rock is short and easily top-roped.

280
El Potrero
5.9 (R)

On the extreme left-hand edge of the face, head up past a fixed stopper to the top. Protection on this route is very poor. FA unknown.

281
Zyzzxx
Difficult 5th

Ascend the left side of the wall.
FA unknown

282
Pro Job
5.9+ TR

Just left of *Miccis*. Climb up and traverse right under the second bolt of *Miccis*. FA unknown.

283
Miccis
★★ 5.9

(aka: Chemain de Paix) Follow pockets and bolts to the top. Originally done on a TR. Additional bolts have been added since the first ascent.
FA Bruce Hendricks and Carol Wiede, February 1982.

284
Menage a Trois
★★★ 5.10b

In the middle of the wall, follow a seam past bolts directly to the top. Wired stoppers are helpful to take along.
FA Henry Barber and Yvon Chouinard, mid-1970's.

The first ascent party lead the route without the bolts being in place.

284a: Just to the left of the 5.10's start, climb face holds (5.9) up and then right to the second bolt on the 5.10 route.
FA unknown.

Potrero John Wall and Practice Rock

285
Rubber Man
★ ★ **5.10+ TR**
Right of *Menage a Trois* thin face climbing leads past a thin ledge diagonalling up and right. Five bolts protect the route; crux moves are at the first and third bolts. FA unknown.

Practice Rock

286
Beginnings
★ **5.4**
From the ground, climb up past the large hole. Step right, then following the cracks, head directly to the top. FA unknown.

The Fortress

To the right (upstream), near the highway bridge, is a group of triangular slabs broken by gullies and pine trees. The "Fortress" was climbed as early as the mid-1960's but nobody seems to be keeping track of what they've done there.

Dave Abeloe climbing Terror of the Greeks. *Photo: Matthew Kerwin.*

Pine Mountain Inn

287
Terror of the
Greeks
★ 5.10

This slanting crack is just north and across the road from the Pine Mountain Inn on Highway 33. The route starts with a horizontal off-width and protection tends to get easier the further you climb. FA Dave Abeloe and friend, late 1970's.

Point Mugu

There are several established routes on the ocean side of the hill one hundred yards west of Mugu Rock. The formation lies on the coast, along Highway 1, just south of Point Mugu Naval Air Station.

The cliff sits beyond the old fence-lined roadway just above the shore. Several routes, ranging in difficulty from 5.7 to hard 5.11 ascend the often crumbly face. All of the single pitch routes end at the broken ledges and loose slabs partway up the hillside. A small selection of nuts, including medium sizes, is suggested.

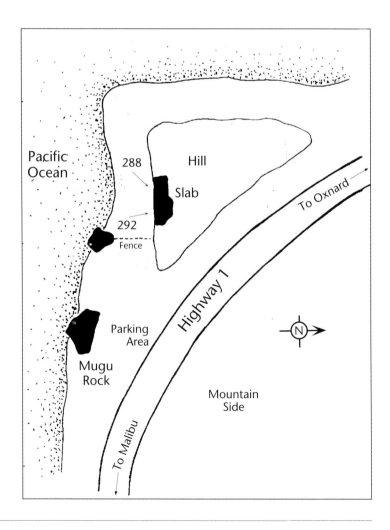

All of the following routes lie on the cleanest slab area between a dark intrusion on the left and a broken area on the right.

288
Finger Crack
5.8

Left-most crack higher on the face. Ascend from the lower section via either the broken edges and ramps in the middle of the face or from the right leaning edges and crack starting at the left side of the wall. FA unknown.

289
Inverted Staircase
5.9 TR

Just left of center, an inverted, jagged ramp heads up and left. Climb directly up through the center of this feature to the ledge partway up the face. Finish via either the *Finger Crack* or the *Parallel Cracks*. FTR unknown.

290
Parallel Cracks
5.7

By way of either start variation mentioned in the *Finger Crack* route, climb the parallel cracks just left of the obvious right-facing dihedral in the middle of the upper wall. FA unknown.

291
Dihedral Route
5.8

Climb the obvious right-facing dihedral in the middle of the wall to fixed anchor bolts. Suggest rappelling from here. FA unknown.

292
Bolt Route
5.11+

Climb the right leaning line of bolts on the right-hand side of the slab to the top. Beware of loose rock near the top. FA unknown.

Conejo Mountain

Between Camarillo and Thousand Oaks, take the Wendy Drive exit from Highway 101. Head south on Wendy Drive, then turn right (west) onto Old Conejo Road. Follow Old Conejo Road to where it ends at a gate. Conejo Wall and Outcast wall are found by hiking up the dirt road past the gate.

Conejo Wall

This is the short, 35 foot high wall overlooking the trailer park.

293
Conejo
5.11b

Climb past four bolts on the lowest, left-most portion of the face. The line sports small edges and shallow pockets typical of the areas volcanic formations. Two-bolt top anchor.
FA Stuart Ruckman, spring 1993.

Outcast Wall

After about a 45 minute walk up the dirt road (2-3 miles), a low dome of rock will be seen on the right, below the road. A short distance further down the road the main 60 foot high wall can be seen. New routes in this area have needed a lot of cleaning. All the noted routes can be easily set up as top-ropes.

294
Junk Bonds
★ 5.12c

Left-most route on cliff. Climbs out a bulge to a sustained head-wall. Crux between the third and fourth bolts. Seven bolts total, plus top anchors.
FA Stuart Ruckman, spring 1993.

295
The Outcast
★ 5.12a

Climb straight up the middle of the wall on shallow pockets. Protected by six bolts, this is the best of the three listed routes.
FA Stuart Ruckman, spring 1993.

296
Cowgirl Paradise
★ 5.11b

Right-most line on the cliff. Good pockets lead past seven bolts. The crux is at the last bolt.
FA Stuart Ruckman, spring 1993.

Ventura Bouldering

There are numerous bouldering opportunities at Thacher School, Foothill Crag, and Shelf Ridge. Refer to those sections elsewhere in the book.

Camarillo Grove Park ★ ★

Drive south of Camarillo on Highway 101. Take the Camarillo Springs offramp to Camarillo Grove Park. Drive straight through the park to the parking field. (There is an entrance fee). Out across the field and sitting in the bushes is an excellent large boulder. The rock is not sandstone, but volcanic in origin. The boulder provides high quality face climbing.

Note: Access to the boulder at Camarillo Grove Park is somewhat questionable (it may require crossing private property), therefore it would be best to check with the rangers at the park before climbing there.

Mugu Rock ★ ★ ★

North of Camarillo Grove Park on Highway 101, take the Las Posas Road turnoff west to Highway 1. Head south on Highway 1. Within a few miles, the road makes a sweep around a point. You'll see a large boulder covered with graffiti on the ocean side of the highway. Mugu Rock has a number of excellent crack and face climbs of bouldering and top-rope height. Be prepared to put up with spectators and traffic noise. (See also page 175.)

Pine Mountain ★

The dirt road out onto Pine Mountain above Sespe leads to decent bouldering. Turn east from Highway 33 onto a dirt road at Pine Mountain Summit (north of Sespe Gorge and the Pine Mountain Inn). Follow the dirt road for several miles along the ridge until you see the boulders.

*Doug Hsu at
Camarillo Grove Park.
Photo: Gary Tabor*

San Luis Obispo

"There is something surprising in the tranquility of this deserted landscape where once...volcanoes boomed to each other in their subterrainian organs and spat forth their fire. ...the slopes are gentle; one forgets the travail that gave them birth."

—Wind, Sand and Stars
by Antoine de Saint Exupery

S an Luis Obispo marks the northern realm of climbing in the tri-counties. Santa Barbara and San Luis Obispo are separated by approximately a two hour drive along Highway 101.

The rock of San Luis Obispo provides the tri-county climber with a refreshing change from the usual sandstone formations found elsewhere along the south coast. The rock, volcanic in origin, lends itself to a variety of intriguing features—from pockets to cracks to wild patterns of "tiger stripe" edges. Take a look at the base of the Cracked Wall on Bishop's Peak to see geology in action...

Most of the climbing is done on the various crags that make up Bishop's Peak. The remainder of the routes are scattered among the "Sister" peaks to the west. There is also climbing to be found on a few other isolated formations in the SLO backcountry.

The volcanic peaks of the Seven Sisters are, from southeast to northwest: Cerro San Luis Obispo (aka: Madonna Peak), Bishop's Peak, Chumash Peak, Cerro Romauldo, Hollister Peak, Cerro Cabrillo, and Morro Rock. These peaks contain the greatest concentration of quality rock faces in San Luis Obispo County.

As of this writing Cuesta Rock is closed to climbing. Hollister Peak is on private land and climbing is frowned upon by the owners. Chumash Peak and Cerro Romualdo are also off limits. Morro Rock has been closed for years to climbing due to its being the home of the peregrine falcon which is an endangered species.

This currently leaves Bishop's Peak and Cerro Cabrillo as the major options for the climber.

There has been talk of creating a preserve or park out of the Seven Sisters and the slopes surrounding them. Any assistance you can lend to making this proposal a reality would not only help add a great asset to the community but to climbers' access as well.

Opposite page: Pete Gulyash leading
The Hanging Teeth. *Photo: Jim Gilpin*

Local standards have been, and remain very high. This is evident in the fact that almost all bolted routes to date have had the protection placed on lead (and mostly on-sight). The frequent long lead-outs display a high degree of boldness and commitment. A local "rule" is to leave any established route protection as is. Do not add or remove any fixed protection found on a route unless it has deteriorated to the point of needing replacement.

In comparison with many other climbing areas, SLO is kept extremely clean of trash; the amount of chalk evident on the boulders below Bishop's has been minimal as well.

San Luis Obispo has an abundance of poison oak. A veritable plethora of these three-leafed plants abounds all about the base of Bishop's and elsewhere. Watch where you walk.

Most of the property surrounding these peaks is private farm land and closure of any and all the climbing areas could result if fences are damaged, rocks are defaced, private property not respected, and trash tossed about.

Bishop's Peak

The center of climbing in San Luis Obispo, Bishop's Peak, is composed of a number of small crags and rock walls.

Cracked Wall, P-Wall and Shadow Wall are the three primary rock faces with a host of high quality routes. Above, below, and to the sides are a number of smaller formations with equal quality but shorter routes. Many of the lesser outcrops have difficult approaches.

A selection of protection up to two inches along with a handful of runners should be enough gear for most routes.

From Highway 101 take the Highway 1, Morro Bay exit. Head north toward Morro Bay and turn left (west) onto Highland Drive. Park at the end of Highland Drive. Specific approach information can be found under each of the formation headings.

Bishop's Peak

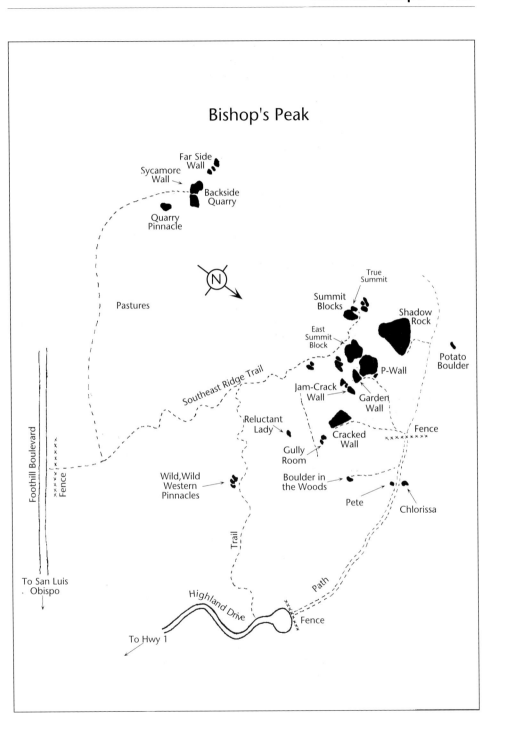

Bishop's Peak

Shadow Rock

P-Wall

Summit Blocks

Garden Wall

Jam Crack Wall

Cracked Wall

Reluctant Lady

Path to Highland Drive

The Wild, Wild Western Pinnacles

(aka: Orange Rocks) The cluster of 40 foot pinnacles on the south flank of Bishop's Peak just above the Highland Drive parking area. All routes are on the southeast faces. Approach via the Oak Tree Trail. Hike up into the quarried area, then scramble up the loose gully behind the pinnacles. Rap down.

297
High Noon
★★ **5.10d**

Climb past three bolts on the upper main pillar to the top. A 5.10 variation exists above and right of the first bolt with a small mantel ledge. Just before the second bolt you need to be careful making a friction move. Bring nuts for the top anchor. FTR Mark Joillof and Ed Keefe, 1990.
FA Pete Gulyash and Ed Keefe, 1990.

298
Harlot's Slot
5.11 TR

From a boulder start the climb proceeds directly up the left side of the central pillar. FTR Pete Gulyash and Ed Keefe, 1990.

299
Poker
5.10 TR

Ascends the larger, lower pillar with a roof at half-height. Several variations exist with the crux at the roof. Single bolt on top of the pinnacle. FA Pete Gulyash and Ed Keefe, 1990.

300
Unnamed Route
5.8 TR

A nebulous route to the right of *Poker*. This may best be approached by skirting the base. FA unknown.

Gully Room

There is a narrow corridor between blocky cracked boulders in a gully 200 feet from the summit ridge to the east of Cracked Wall. The best approach is from the ridge above.

301
Corridor Crack
★ **5.10b**

A fist crack in the corridor on the uphill boulder.
FA Barry Frantz and Pete Gulyash, February 1987.

302
East Cracks
5.6

Wide cracks on east face of the lowest block in the corridor.
FA unknown.

303
Reluctant Lady
5.8

An enjoyable climb on a 25 foot pinnacle with a lousy approach. Sits on a ridge above the gully east of Cracked Wall and Imaginary Boulder. Ascend the uphill arete of this remarkably balanced blade of rock. FA Jim Gilpin and Lee Millon, 1983.

Cracked Wall

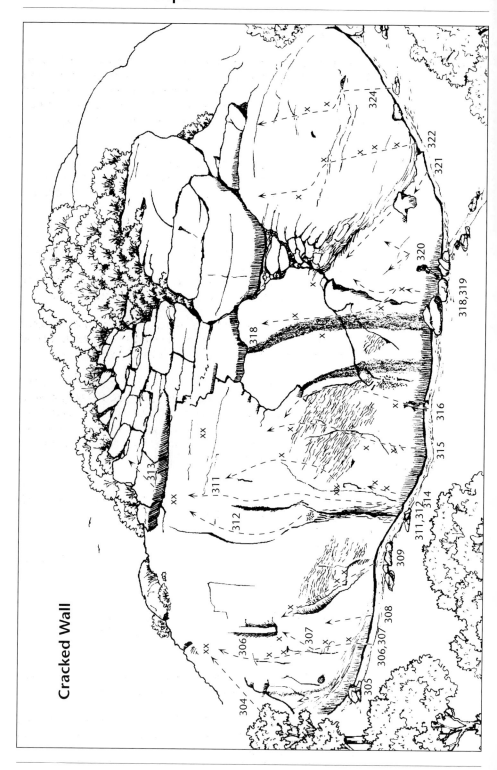

Pinnacles Area

Imaginary Boulder: Hidden in the brush about 100 feet downhill and left of Cracked Wall. There are several short 5.9 and 5.10 crack and face routes. A faint trail leads from Cracked Wall to the top of this small, hard to see crag. Routes were established by Ken Klis, Chris Moes, Ivan Jasenovic and Craig Tatum in 1987.

A second minor outcrop lies further left along the hillside and across the gully from Imaginary Boulder. It can be distinguished by a three foot wide split or chimney down the middle.

Cracked Wall

From the two large boulders (Chlorissa and Pete) passed on the way to P-Wall, hang a left just after climbing over the fence and head up and left into the woods. The trail will bring you to the right side of Cracked Wall. Routes are described left to right.

There are many route variations on this popular wall. Descent is via a walk off to the left (be careful with loose rocks). A good assortment of protection is needed for these routes.

Pete Gulyash remembers one the first ascents done here..."60 Minutes *was a spur of the moment deal. I met Mark (Perko) to boulder and he said we should go up to Cracked Wall to do something easy. So we went up there... and pulled off this route. I led. It was buried in dirt and lichen. I ate a lot of both. By the time I got to the top I was very camouflaged.*"

304
Chopped Bolt
5.7 TR

On the far left side, climb the ramp up and left of the black streak. FTR Colin Berry and friend, 1981.

305
Arete
★ 5.9+

Ascend the black streak to the blocky arete and continue up. FA unknown.

306
Humps
★★★ 5.11a

Climb *Camel* to its second bolt. Jog up and left to an arching seam with two bolts to the right. Runout at the top. FTR Matt Dancy, 1988. FFA Flint Thorne, 1989.

306a. 5.11: Stay left of the seam on the lower part of *Camel*. FTR Tim Medina, spring 1990. FFA Ryan Bello, spring 1992.

306b. Humping Camel, 5.11: Climb over the bulge between *Humps* and *Camel*. FTR Flint Thorne, Spring 1990; FFA Tim Medina, Spring 1990.

307
Camel
★★★ **5.10b**

Climb up the face past three bolts into a square trough (bring nuts to protect the trough). Named after the musical group. FA Pete Gulyash and Dwight Kroll September, 1980.

308
Slimy Slit
5.10c TR

Climb the face to the right of the bolts on *Camel,* to the square trough above. FA unknown.

309
No Permit Required
★ **5.10b**

Starting under the bulge, climb the small left-facing corner to a bolt. Follow the seam left to a second bolt, then up through ripples. Continue into the square trough mentioned in *Camel.* FA Pat Meezan and Ken Klis, 1985.

310
Unknown
5.9

Climb the face between *No Permit Required* and *60 Minutes.* Questionable pro. FA a Bulgarian mountaineer named Valentino.

311
60 Minutes
★ **5.8+**

(aka: Dead Rat Crack) Climb the obvious large, wide blocky crack to the top. *This route was originally named after the dead rat the first ascensionists found in it.* FA Bob Garing and Rusty Garing, 1970. FFA Pete Gulyash and Mark Perko, July 1985.

312
60 Seconds Over Soledad
★★ **5.6**

Climb the same wide, blocky crack but move into the left fork (black fork) about 30 feet off the ground. Continue to the top. FA unknown.

313
Farewell to Arms
5.9

This climb goes through the roof above the *Sixty Seconds* belay.Very dirty. Bring a large nut. Better yet, don't do it. FA Tim Sorenson, Pete Gulyash and Larry Lepovitz, mid-1981.

314
Western Airlines
★★ **5.11b**

Just right of *60 Minutes* climb up the shield-sized plate past two bolts and follow the seam up to double bolts where you step right onto the obvious "tiger-stripes." Continue straight up past a 4th bolt. *The double bolts are the remains of an old aid line that traversed the entire Cracked Wall. The double bolts were a belay...* FA Erik Erikson and Pete Gulyash, mid-1984.

Opposite: Lee Millon on Camel.
Photo:
Pete Gulyash

314a. 5.11b: Rather than stepping right onto the "tiger-stripes" continue straight up the face above to the 4th bolt. FA unknown.

314b. Left Variation 5.11+: From the double bolts step left and climb straight up the face. FTR John Merriam, June 1990.

315
Curly Shuffle
★★5.11d/5.12a

This climbs the face past two bolts and into the middle of the "tiger-stripes." A small nut protects further moves before the third bolt. FTR Erik Erikson, 1984. FA Tim Medina, spring 1990.

316
The Only Way to Fly
★5.10d

Climb between the tiger stripes and a wide black streak past a bolt on oatmeal-textured rock. From a short diagonal crack, move up and right to a shallow scoop. From the shallow scoop a mantel leads to easier climbing and a chain belay.
FA Dwight Kroll and Anders, August 1978.

317
Jettstream
5.12-

Clip the first bolt on *The Only Way to Fly* then step right, to the right-leaning slot/crack. It is possible to place pro in the beginning of the slot.
FA John Merriam, February 1990.

318
Love in an Elevator
5.10c (R)

Climb to the crux of *Civilized Evil* and traverse left to a bolt in a lumpy bulge. Above the bulge head up a right slanting crack, then left past another bolt to a short headwall with another bolt. Ascend the headwall (crux). Climb over the roof above to the belay of *Curly Shuffle*. FA Menzo Baird and Ed Keefe, 1989.

319
Civilized Evil
★★5.10a

Start 12 feet right of the black streak, below a right-facing blocky corner. Climb up past a bolt and into the corner. It's possible to finish via *Dirty Rats*.
FA Ralston Rutabago (Tim Sorenson), Pete Gulyash, Matt Mesa, and Colin Berry, February 1981.

320
Guides Area
5.5 - 5.9 TR

The thirty feet between *Civilized Evil* and *Dirty Rat's Crack* is host to a number of top-roped problems. FA's unknown.

321
Dirty Rat's Crack
★★5.4

Climb the very obvious large, left-leaning ramp and ledges to roofs. Move around the roof as soon as possible then follow a crack up and right past mantels. Finish in the trees or traverse far to the left to avoid bush whacking. FA unknown.

322
Crank You
Thank You
★★5.11b

Just right of the start to *Dirty Rat's Crack* climb straight up past 4 bolts. The crux is a hard crank over a wave. From the fourth bolt traverse along a ramp up and left to a bolt and then head straight up and right to the top.
FA Tim Sorenson and Pete Gulyash, January 1981.

Erik Erikson on the first ascent of Western Airlines. Photo: Pete Gulyash

"...Tim and I then teamed up to do Lama and Crank You Thank You. We did them on back-to-back weekends as I recall, though for the life of me I can't remember which went first.

Anyway, Tim led both. One afternoon we set out to do Lama. I remember thinking that we were going to get caught by darkness because the bolting was going to take so long. But no... Tim flashed the route, bolting on lead. No hesitations, no false starts, no falls. He climbed it like he had done it 100 times. He even stood on the ledge near the top, unanchored, while he hauled up some nuts to protect the top move. Within the hour the thing was done."

—Pete Gulyash

323
Thank You
Crank You
★ 5.11c

A variation to *Crank You Thank You* using the same bolts but climbing on the right side.
FTR Mark Perko and Pete Gulyash, 1986.
FA Ken Klis, (date unknown).

324
Lama
★ ★ ★ 5.10b

Ten feet further right. Climb up using small pockets to a ledge. Continue past two bolts and climb the thin crack through the roof. At the second bolt move left five feet, at the roof move back five feet.
FA Tim Sorenson and Pete Gulyash, January 1981.

324a Bob's Cling, 5.10b TR: Enter *Lama* via the horizontal seams to the right, bypassing the bottom face moves. At the second bolt climb straight up.
FTR Bob Little and Mike Jablonski, 1988.

John Merriam climbing Jettstream.
Photo: Steve Tucker

Pinnacle-dom Rock

(aka: Owl's Perch) This small formation is located above Cracked Wall. Approach is via the slope just past either the left or (better) right side of Cracked Wall.

325
Huck-a-Mo
★ 5.12a

On the overhanging southeast face. FA Ken Klis, 1989.

326
K-B Trip
5.10a

Located on a low-angle slab immediately behind the pinnacle. The route begins on the left side of the slab in orange rock. A boulder start leads through two bolts. Two top-rope variations exist. FA Ed Keefe and Don Bergan, 1988.

The following routes lie on the small unnamed formation to the right of Pinnacle-Dom Rocks and 150 feet up and left of the Sgt. Peppers route on the Jam Crack Wall.

327
Ivan's Route
★★ 5.11a

Slightly overhanging face on the left side of the north face. FTR Ivan Jasinovich, Bob Little and John Merriam, 1988.

328
Rovert
★ 5.10b

Climb slanted crack to black streak. FA Trevor Perry, 1988.

329
Y-Crack
5.6

To the right of Rovert. FA Chris Moes and Ken Klis, 1986

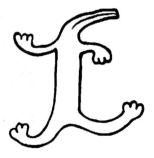

Garden Wall, Jam-Crack Wall

Approaches:

From the parking area at the end of Highland Drive, hop the wooden fence at the end of the pavement. Follow the dirt road north along the hillside past a pond (often dry) to a pair of large boulders (Chlorissa and Pete). Just uphill from the boulders, climb over the fence via a step-ladder. Head up and left along a path through the woods to the left side of P-Wall. All routes on P-Wall are easily accessible from here. To reach the Garden Wall and Jam-Crack Wall, head left from the left base of P-Wall. Garden Wall is the first low angle convoluted and vegetated slab you'll reach. Continue left to reach the Jam-Crack Wall which has an obvious clean crack *(Sgt. Pepper's)*.

Garden Wall

330
Garden 'O' Weedin'
5.6

Located on the left-hand side of the slab (about 75 feet left of main "P" rock). Climb up 80 feet via a right facing corner to a flake traverse right and up to a bolt belay. Mostly 5.2 but the crux is 5.6. FA Craig Griffith, date unknown.

331
Look Ma, No Hands
5.7

Clip the first bolt of *Madison Square Garden* and climb past a short right-facing corner on the left. Two more bolts lead to the belay. FA Joe Potter, and Ryan Bello, 1989.

332
Madison Square
Garden
★ ★ 5.6

Begin in the center of the face atop the highest ground and head for the corner and a bolt. Ascend the corner to a diagonal seam (bring nuts). Climb up and left past several more bolts to the top. FA Pete Gulyash and Karl Gulyash, February 1982.

333
Wandering Woofs of
a Saint Bernard
5.8

Begin at the right-hand side of the slab. The crux moves ascend a small headwall with a bolt on top. Head for the third bolt of *Madison Square Garden* and on to the top. FA Joe Potter (solo), 1989.

Jam-Crack Wall

334
Fester Finger
5.11a TR

This route is 15 feet left of *Sgt. Peppers*. Lieback a diagonal seam on an overhanging wall to a fingertip jam. Continue straight up. FTR Hans Florine and Mike Lopez, 1987.

335
Sgt. Pepper's Lonely
Hearts Hand Jam
★★5.10a

A clean hand and fist crack. Jam the overhang to variations both left and right on the face above. FA Tobin Sorenson (solo), date unknown. *This route originally had a large chockstone in the crack that has since been scandalously removed. Soloed on the first ascent, Mike Cirone later added a bolt. A climber once spent half an hour hanging from his wedged elbow after a fall at the crux.*

P-Wall

Approach as for Garden Wall and Jam Crack Wall. Named for the large painted "P" gracing its upper main face, this wall is home to several tri-county classics. P-Wall and Cracked Wall are probably the most popular climbing spots in San Luis Obispo county.

John Hanna (from the former Hanna's Hardware) along with a fellow named Stewart and 4 Navy sailors fresh home from the war are responsible for painting the "P" in 1946. The original idea was Stewart's. The Navy guys had plenty of rope experience from hanging over the side of their ship to paint the hull. They used a bosun's chair to move up, down and around while John and Stewart tended the ropes and anchors. It took them a full day.

They used 10 gallons of white lead and 5 of black lead. The paint was donated by Chevron where one of the Navy guys worked. Dirty and covered with poison oak, they and their wives went out to Cuesta Park that evening for a big blow-out Bar-B-Que to celebrate (their survival probably).

They were a bit afraid that the principal of Cal Poly, Julian McPhee, might not take to the new "P" but as it turned out, the "P" was no "P"roblem.

336
Pages
5.10TR

This route is on the far left side of the left face. The start is from the uppermost part of the gully. FTR Nate Sears, Chris Moes, and Ken Klis, 1987.

East Summit Blocks

356 357

Walk-Off

Walk-Off

xx

xx

339

xx

343

348

341

349

351

337

x

348

xx

344

x

340

x

341

342

x

xx

346

350

352

353
354
355

338

Pinnacle

339

341

345

346

Trail to Garden
and Jamb Crack
Walls

P-Wall

337
Stage Fright
★★★ 5.9+ (R)

Start at a right-leaning ramp below and left of a bolt. Climb past the bolt then up and left to a second bolt below an under-cling. Move up and right to a third bolt below a bulge, step left and wander up and left to the top. A good route.
FA Tim Sorenson and Jeff Shrimpton, February 1981.

338
Indecent Exposure
★ 5.7

Twelve feet downhill from *Stage Fright*, climb up to the promi-nent large chockstone in the left-leaning ramp. Mantel up and right to the first bolt. Awkward moves up and left and then back right to the second bolt. Traverse over to the *P-Crack* belay, crossing a bolt on *Out of Hangers* on the way.
FA James Blench, date unknown.

339
Out of Hangers
★★★ 5.10b (R)

Follow the obvious arete just left of *Impacted Stool Crack*. Face climb straight up past 5 bolts for a full pitch, staying on the arete. This route ends on the same ledge as *Stage Fright*. Another good route, on-sight flashed with bolts placed on lead. Bring your own hangers just in case.
FA Tim Sorenson and Jeff Shrimpton, February 1981.

340
Impacted Stool Crack
★★★ 5.9+ (R)

From the base of the left side of P-Wall, climb up to the short crack above. A serious runout after the first bolt above the crack, most people traverse right to *P-Crack*.
FA Richard Harrison, date unknown.

341
P-Crack
★★★ 5.8+

Climb the prominent crack just right of *Impacted Stool Crack*. After the first bolt when the crack ends, climb up and right to a second bolt, then up and back left towards the belay bolts above. FA unknown, pre-1970 via direct aid.
FFA Rusty Garing and Chip Barclay, 1971.

341a. 5.10c ★★ Climb straight past the first bolt to the belay rather than moving right to the second bolt. A missing bolt makes this an exciting lead.
FA unknown. FFA Rusty Garing and Chip Barclay, 1972.

341b. 5.11b ★ Climb up and to the left of the first bolt.
FA unknown.

342
Black Streak
5.10a (R)

A few feet right of *P-Crack*, climb up the black water streak past 3 bolts to connect with the belay above *P-Crack*.
FA Menzo Baird and Ed Keefe, 1989.

343
Letterman
★ 5.6

From the belay above *P-Crack* climb up and right to a roof. Climb over the roof to an obvious crack which heads up and left across the "P." FA Colin Berry and friend, 1982.

344
Jump for Joy
★★ 5.9 (R)

From the chain belay at the base of *P-Crack,* move right into a large bowl then up the right side of the bowl 15 feet to a bolt. Climb 40 feet past a second bolt to an alcove by the "P." FA Ed Sampson, Mike Cirone, and James Blench, August 1979.

345
The Hanging Teeth
★★ 5.8 (R)

Start at the top of a pedestal behind the oak tree and climb past two bolts to a large undercling. Move right under the undercling and climb up to a right facing book. Continue past two more bolts to a large left facing corner and the belay above. FA Gregg Cassabarth and Rusty Garing, 1971.

346
P-Wall Direct
★★ 5.8

Just to the right of the oak tree, climb up to a bolt just below a small roof in the obvious black streak in the middle of the wall. The first bolt was placed after the first ascent. Climb right to short double cracks and continue up into a black streak clipping bolts on the second pitch of *Rusty's Cave.* You can also connect with the finish of *The Hanging Teeth.* FA Mike Cirone and Ed Sampson March, 1977.

Reported as this book went to press: Slime n' Dine, 5 bolts, 5.10c. *FA Ryan Bello and Matt Luck, 1993.*

347
Flinging Moss at the
Molson Belay
5.10c TR

Start at the left side of the notch between the detached block (pinnacle) and the wall. Climb left and up into a bowl then straight up to the bolt anchors. FTR Rick Harlan, Mark Perko and Pete Gulyash, 1985.

348
Cave Route
★ 5.6

(aka: Cave to P) From the cave, head left to connect with *The Hanging Teeth.* This route was originally done in combination with *Rusty's Cave* as a two pitch route. FA Joe Zimmerman, Bob Garing, and Rusty Garing, 1970.

On the rappel from the first ascent, Rusty Garing remembers his dad (Bob Garing) lecturing him to place more than a single Bong piton for a rap anchor. Dad was right... the Bong popped as they started down the ropes, and only the additional pitons they'd placed saved them from plunging to the ground.

Opposite: Pete Gulyash leading P-Crack.
Photo: Doug Guillot

349
Biemer's Trough
★ **5.7 (R)**

From the cave, climb up into a trough out of *Rusty's Cave* and continue to the top.
FA Don Biemer and Ed Sampson, February 1975.

350
Rusty's Cave
★★★ **5.8**

From the left side of the notch climb up the large blocky crack. After 50 feet traverse left past a bolt to the cave.
FA Unknown. FFA Rusty Garing.

351
Energy Crisis
★ **5.9 (R)**

Start at *Rusty's Cave* and continue straight up the crack past bulges instead of traversing left. Can be tricky getting good pro at the crux. Continue up and left, running it out to two bolts at the top. FA Paul Clarke and Ed Sampson, July 1976.

352
Spring Route
5.8

From the notch, move up and right on large holds around the arete to a small roof. A bolt protects the move over the roof. Continue straight up following a shallow groove.
FA unknown.

352a. ★★ Dyno Dog 5.10: Two routes start side by side to the right of the true *Spring Route*. The left route is slightly harder and stays left of the arete for the last 15 feet.
FA Ed Keefe and Ryan Bello, early 1990.

352b. ★★★ Leapin' Lizards 5.8: The right-hand route utilizes several fantastic pockets. Ascend either line of three bolts to the two-bolt belay below the *Spring Route* roof.
FA Ed Keefe and Ryan Bello, early 1990.

353
Free For All
5.11+

Climb the original aid route up the gully to the right of *Spring Route*. Stay right of the bolts and climb over the roof and through bolts above. FFA Ryan Bello and Dave Bevan, April, 1992.

354
Motor Mouth
5.6

A dirty route that follows a large left facing corner 30 feet uphill from *Aid Route*. The route starts under a large overhang and ends way above *Rusty's Cave*. Follow the crack under the left-leaning overhang (watch for rope drag).
FA Ed Sampson and friends, August 1976.

355
Whistling Blocks
5.6

A short distance uphill from *Motor Mouth,* a crack parallels the ground about eight feet overhead. Belay when possible and continue along the crack to a poor stance with vegetation and poor bolts. FA Ed Keefe, Pete Gulyash and Bob Little, 1990.

Upper P-Wall

The following routes lie on the short, low-angle slab above and slightly right of P-Wall. These routes are fun but not highly recommended.

356
Grotto
5.6

On the left-hand side of the slab a bolt protects an overhang at the top of the route. There are a total of three bolts on the route. FA Ed Keefe, Pete Gulyash, 1990.

357
Avoidance
5.6

On the right-hand side of the slab, pass a bolt on the right. Above the bolt, continue climbing, staying just left of the arete. About fifty feet up, a bolt protects a move past a headwall. Easier climbing leads to a bolt anchor. FA Ed Keefe, Pete Gulyash, 1990.

Crux moves of Rusty's Cave, *Pete Gulyash climbing.*
Photo: Mark Perko

Shadow Rock

From the boulders (Chlorissa and Pete) described in the approach to P-Wall, head over the step-ladder on the fence. Continue on the path up the hill to the right. At a point where the path starts to dip down the hill look for a trail heading up through the trees to the base of the most classic slab formation in the tri-counties. When descending, there is a real danger of rappelling off the end of your rope, when you use only one rope to rappel. Be careful!

Shadow Rock was first climbed via aid techniques (the Shadow route) by Waters and Russell around 1970. Be aware that many of the older bolts show signs of aging.

358
THC
5.10b (R)

This is the highest line of bolts far up the gully that forms the left side of the formation. Climb up past two bolts staying left toward the top for a 5.10 route. Five feet to the right it's not quite so hard. FA Ken Klis and Pat Meezan, 1988.

359
Swallow
5.7 (R)

Twelve feet down the gully from the start of *THC*, follow natural features to a hole. From the highest hole climb straight up a headwall then wander to the highest belay. FA Colin Berry and Pete Gulyash, March 1982.

360
First Offense
★★ 5.10b

Start at the base of the obvious small oak tree in the gully. Follow the line of bolts. FA Ryan Bello and Joe Potter, 1990.

361
Easy Street
5.6 (R)

This line is very obscure; you never really know if you're on it. Start at the base of the short steep wall below the oak tree. Climb over the headwall just right of a bolt. Traverse out onto the face to a one inch crack. Follow the crack up and left protecting with nuts for about 120 feet to the two-bolt belay of *Swallow* (poor protection). FA James Blench, pre-1978.

362
Three to Get Ready
5.8

From the nice, flat belay stance 20 feet below the oak tree, climb up and follow the bolts to the belay of *Thin Man*. This a very straight line from bottom to top. (Note that this belay is below and to the right of the *Swallow* belay). This is a full pitch. FA Menzo Baird and Ed Keefe, 1989.

Shadow Rock

363
Thin Man
★ ★ **5.9 (R)**

This is the last line on the left just before heading up the gully. Start from the ground or traverse in to the first bolt. Follow bolts straight up to the top. There is a long runout between the third and fourth bolt (about 40 feet of 5.6).
FA Ed Sampson and Mike Cirone, October 1977.

364
Inner Sanctum
★ ★ **5.10a (R)**

Two bolts protect a full length pitch with the first bolt 35 feet off the ground above 5.8 moves. Seeing as how Tobin lead the FA we should be happy there are any bolts at all.
FA Tobin Sorenson and Ed Sampson, pre-1977.

365
Pressure Drop
★ **5.10b (R)**

Start on the left-hand side of the pedestal mentioned in *Shadow*. From the pedestal climb up and left a bit then straight up. The original route had two bolts and traversed to the *Shadow* belay on the right.
FA John Merriam and Bob Little, June 1988.

365a. Pressure Drop Direct 5.10b (R): A third bolt was added continuing the line directly up to the upper belay.
FA Ken Klis and Nate Sears, 1989.

366
Shadow
★ ★ ★ **5.8**

Start on the left side of the pedestal as for *Pressure Drop*, moving right after 12 feet to follow the line of bolts left of the overlap. A direct start variation heads up from directly under the first bolt.
FA Waters and Russel, 1970.
FFA Probably Ed Sampson, before 1978.

This was the first route on the formation and many of the old aid bolts were removed by Ed when the line went free. As a side note, two climbers popped off the second pitch and went all the way to the ground when a single belay bolt pulled.

367
I Love a Mystery
5.10 (R)

Start on the right side of the *Shadow* pedestal. Climb up about seven feet past a dish and traverse left to *Shadow*, clip the first bolt and traverse back to continue up to the first belay. The original line went without bolts although the bolts on *Lycra* are now used for protection, essentially blending the two routes.
FA Mike Cirone, October 1977.

368
Lycra
★ ★ **5.10a**

(aka: Petty Larceny) Meant to be a separate route from *I Love a Mystery*, this variant is now the accepted line. It starts several feet right of *I Love a Mystery* and climbs past a bolt and a large pocket (large cam) before continuing past the bolts above.
FA Colin Berry and friend, March 1982.

369
Battle of the Bulge
★ ★ **5.10c**

An obvious bulge right of *Lycra* (25 feet right of *Shadow*). Climb directly up the center of the bulge, protected by a bolt. After a difficult mantel move on top of the bulge continue to the second bolt on *Diamond*. If you stay on the left side of the bulge it's 5.10c. FTR Rick Harlan and Lee Millon, February 1980.
FA Pete Gulyash and Lee Millon, one week later, 1980.

Libby Whaley leading Shadow. *Photo: Steve Tucker*

370
Diamond
★ ★ **5.9 (R)**

Six feet right of *Battle of the Bulge* climb to the bolt just above the two inch overhang. Continue up (possibly traversing left and back—use your judgement) to two more bolts at the top of *Shadow*. This is a full length pitch.
FA Mike Cirone and Ed Sampson, pre-1978.

371
Desperado
★ ★ **5.10d**

Ten feet right of *Diamond* climb up past the large hole to the first bolt. Move left and climb up past three more bolts. Traverse left below the shrubbery and connect with *Diamond*.
FA Larry Lepovitz and Pete Gulyash, October 1980.

Summit Blocks

The large boulders at the summit of Bishop's Peak have a number of short, diverse routes. The climbs range from technical faces to chimneys. The rock covers the spectrum from solid to rotten. This area is also very popular with weekend hikers.

There are several ways to approach; the easiest, and the longest, is from the parking area off of Foothill Boulevard. Park across from the Baptist church and head uphill for about a 45 minute walk. Approach can also be made from Highland Drive. Any of several trails lead up from the "Wild, Wild Western Pinnacles" area. Another approach is via the central gully to the right of P-Wall. As always, be wary of poison oak.

Many of the routes are on the "sunny" side thus being good choices in colder weather. The summit of Bishop's Peak is split into three blocky areas, the middle of which is the true summit. The eastern blocks see the most activity.

The following are the first of the large summit blocks you will encounter when approaching from Foothill Boulevard:

East Summit Block (South Face)

372
Vance's Vertical Vent
★★ **5.8 (R)**

Climb overhanging moves above the painted "TL" to enter the extremely rotten S-shaped chimney and body-jam to the top. Rarely led. FA Pat Coyes, Rusty Garing, Bob Garing, Rose Garing, Rick Parent, and Chip Barclay, 1970.
FFA Dwight Kroll and Vance Weber, November 1977.

373
Hand Job
★ **5.10c**

20 feet to the right of *Vance's Vertical Vent*, climb the obvious jam crack. Usually top-roped. FA Dwight Kroll and Bob Fuller, January 1978.

374
Hardly Worth the Trouble
★ **5.7**

(aka: Scratch and Sniff) On the tier above/behind *Handjob*, climb the obvious crack in the corner. Good protection in the crack. FA Pat Coyes, Rusty Garing, Bob Garing, Rose Garing, Rick Parent, and Chip Barclay, 1970.
FFA Dwight Kroll and Bob Fuller, January 1978.

East Summit Block—East Face (Above); South Face (Below)

East Summit Block (East Face)

375
Hand Munch
5.9

On the far left side, climb the rotten crack that leads out left under the large block.
FA Dwight Kroll, solo, October 1979.

376
Maria's Crack
★ **5.9**

(aka: If Looks Could Kill) Start as for *Hand Munch* but climb up under the right side of the large block.
FA Dwight Kroll and Vance Weber, March 1978.

377
Moser
★ **5.10c TR**

Climb the face left of *Flakes to Fresno*.
Loose and flaky.
FA Menzo Baird, February 1988.

378
Flakes to Fresno
★ ★ ★ **5.8**

Climb the obvious left leaning crack up the center of the face.
FA Pat Coyes, Rusty Garing, Bob Garing, Rose Garing, Rick Parent, and Chip Barclay, 1970.

379
The Trough
5.9 TR

(aka: Conflicting Interest) Start on *Flakes to Fresno* and traverse out and right to the vertical crease.
FTR unknown, pre-1986.

380
Lim's Cramp Chimney
5.4

Obvious chimney on the right side of the face.
FA Pat Coyes, Rusty Garing, Bob Garing, Rose Garing, Rick Parent, and Chip Barclay, 1970.

381
The Wave
5.10a TR

Climb up the seam on the left side of the roof and continue up.
Another much harder (5.12) variation climbs through the roof itself via the thin crack. Climb the face above. FA unknown.

382
The Seam
★ **5.11a TR**

On a separate boulder 40 feet right (east) of *The Wave*. Several other toperope problems are on this same boulder.
FTR Mark Perko, Erik Erikson, Pete Gulyash, 1986.

383
Flint's Stone
5.12- TR

This route is on the east side of another boulder 50 feet downhill from *The Seam*.
FTR John Merriam, December 1990.

Menzo Baird leading Flakes to Fresno.
Photo: courtesy Menzo Baird.

East Summit Block (Northwest Face)

Approach by traversing left around a corner from *Hand Munch*. A trail drops down the hillside and brings you around to the face.

384
The Lost 'Biner
★ 5.7

This route is located in a huge corner/dihedral. Start at the slab leading to the left leaning ramp. Climb up and left through the blocky features to the blocky, right-facing corner. FA unknown.

385
Turkey Vulture
★ 5.11b

A right leaning, overhanging crack with one bolt higher up. FTR Matt Dancy, 1988. FA Menzo Baird, 1989.

386
Gymnast
5.11a TR

Right of *Turkey Vulture* 40 feet. The route faces southwest. Climb a 30 foot face above small roofs. FA Hans Florine, 1988.

Further downhill and around the corner on the north-east face is a wide crack/chimney:

387
Arriba Su Vientre
5.8

Climb the overhanging, rotten, mossy, dirty, v-shaped, crack/chimney to the top. This one looks really bad—worse than *Farewell to Arms*. At least *Farewell to Arms* is over quickly. FA unknown, pre-1978.

East Summit Block,
Northwest Face

True Summit Block

These routes are under the obvious piercing prow that points south. There is a line of aid bolts leading out under the prow.

388
Meltdown
★★★ **5.11d (R)**

Southwest facing corner, with 4 bolts.
FTR Ryan Bellows, summer 1991.
FA Menzo Baird, summer 1991.

389
The Mickey B. Way
★★ **5.11d**

Offwidth to fist size crack in a cave facing south directly beneath the prow.
FA Pete Gulyash, 1979.

390
Sidewinder
5.10a

Horizontal crack in the block just below and right of the main prow.
FA Ken Klis and Pat Meezan, 1987.

True Summit Blocks

The Backside Quarry

An old rock quarry lies at the base of the west side of Bishop's Peak. The best approach is from the parking area on Foothill Boulevard. Skirt left around the base of Bishop's across the cow pastures until you can see the obvious rock wall and short talus slope. The rock here can be quite loose and shattered. Exercise caution and judgment when climbing here.

The Far Side Wall is a few hundred feet left of the main quarry. The Sycamore Wall is situated on the left side of the quarry directly behind a large sycamore tree.

Far Side Wall
This small crag (80 feet high and 80 feet wide) lies about 250 feet left of the Sycamore Wall behind a large oak tree.

391
Dreams of Rabid Trucks
★★ **5.10b**
A bolt below a short, clean crack marks this route. Above the crack, climb up and right to a vegetated crack below a ledge with two bolts. FA Pete Gulyash, Barry Frantz, 1989.

392
The Far Side
5.9
Mantel a small bulge twenty feet right of the previous route. A bolt 25 feet higher protects steeper rock leading to a vegetated crack and the belay. FA Barry Frantz, Pete Gulyash, 1989.

393
Pharoah's Crack
★ **5.8+**
A couple of hundred yards left of the Far Side Wall is a small cluster of blocks with a nice 25-foot crack. FA Tim Medina, Joe Potter, February 19, 1990.

Sycamore Wall
Distinguished by the large sycamore tree at it's base, this is the left-most slab of the main quarry. All the routes here end at a ledge which can be reached by going up and around the left side of the wall.

394
Barry's Route
5.9TR
Climbs over the bulge to the ledge at the far left side of the Sycamore Wall. FTR Barry Frantz, 1989.

395
Joe's Route
5.8
In the middle of the wall (in front of the Sycamore), climb the face past several bolts. This route is incomplete. FA Joe Potter and partner, 1989.

396
Hedges, Ledges
and Wedges
5.8
Ascend the only crack on this wall. Above the grottoes move out onto the left face and finish the route climbing next to the crack. Good climbing but dirty. FA Mark Perko, Laurie Perko, Pete Gulyash, Barry Frantz, Gil Larson, 1989.

397
Edges, Ledges
and Knobs
5.9+
Begin in the hole behind the blocks 25 feet right of *Hedges, Ledges and Wedges* and face climb past 8 bolts or so. From the sixth bolt traverse left about ten feet to a bolt, then continue up. A variation finishes up and right from the sixth bolt. FTR Pete Gulyash, Barry Frantz, 1988; FA Ken Klis (right-hand finish), 1989.

Quarry Wall

398
No Haps
5.10b
(Unfinished project) On the far right-hand side of the wall, this climb ascends the crack through the large dark blocks and overhangs. A fixed pin is low on the route. The route has not been finished. First attempted by Pete Gulyash and Alan Root, 1981.

Quarry Pinnacle

399
Dare a Dactyl
5.8
Climb the obvious crack to the top of the layered pinnacle. There is no anchor on top, so getting down is interesting. FA Gil Larson, Pete Gulyash, 1988.

Cerro Cabrillo

Chorro Willows West

(aka Back Bay Boulders) Just east of Morro Bay on Highway 1 turn south onto South Bay Blvd. After about 1/2 mile, before the road turns, you will see the large, 40 foot high boulders on the small hill off to the left across the creek. One of the boulders is noticeably overhanging. Park at the locked gate and follow the dirt road and path past an old building. Access is over state owned land across the creek (there are Indian mortar holes on this hill). Beat the brush uphill to the more eastern of the two boulders.

400
Chorro Willows
Overhang
A1

Chorro Willows Overhang is on the northeast side of the rock. The rock has two smooth, rounded ceilings with over a dozen bolts.

FA Jeff Lang and Bruce Cotter, Fall 1975.

401
The Ramp
5.10d

Start at the tree on the same boulder as the bolt ladder and climb up the leaning dike to the top.

FA unknown.

The rock below *The Ramp* has a bolt-protected move to its top. There are several top-rope problems as well.

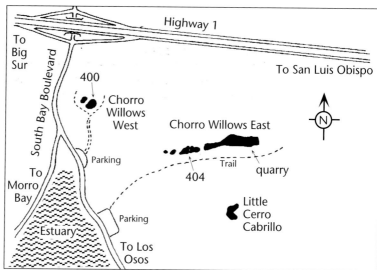

Chorro Willows East

Drive south a few minutes past the Chorro Willows West parking area until you see the small cliffs and boulders on the west flank of Cerro Cabrillo. Park at the dirt area on the left. Good top-roping abounds here. Follow the trail to the left side of the long, low rock wall. The quarry on the right is loose and dangerous. The orangish, overhanging boulder on the hillside to the left has a bolt ladder. The following routes lie on the first obvious alcove area on the main cliff when walking east on the dirt road toward the quarry.

402
Brown Smoothies
5.11TR

Situated on the first small cliff. Look for several bolts on the face left of the alcove.
FA Tim Medina, 1990.

403
Left Arete
5.10b

This is the the obvious buttress just left of the alcove.
FTR Ryan Bellos, 1990.

404
Back Crack
5.8

This is the crack at the back of the first obvious alcove.
FA unknown.

There are about ten top-rope face climbs on the main cliff on either side of the first alcove/buttress area.

Little Cerro Cabrillo

This is the satellite peak across the small valley to the south of Cerro Cabrillo. There are several old bolts on the west facing side of the hill. Route information has yet to be obtained.

Beartrap Spire

Castle Crags

Take highway 101 to the Santa Margarita exit. Drive southeast on Highway 58. Turn onto Pozo Road towards La Panza Camp which is on Forest Service road #M3093. This road cuts through the Machesna Mountain Wilderness and eventually reconnects with Highway 58 in the Carrizo Valley Plain. From La Panza Camp, turn onto Forest Service road #29S18. Follow this road, past Queen Bee Camp, always bearing to the right. Just past Chester Spring (not clearly marked) there is a sharp uphill fork in the road. Drive right on switchbacks towards Pine Mountain.

The road tops out on the main ridge. Park at the trailhead on the left (blocked by a gate made of large diameter pipe). Follow the trail off to the southeast. The formations lie along the north edge of the main ridge. These rocks are part of a series of similar outcrops along Pine Mountain and the La Panza Range.

Beartrap Spire lies further along road #29S18 to the east and is marked on the topographic map as point 2677 ft. It rises from the northern slope of the mountains about two miles southeast of the main ridgeline formations described above.

The rock at Castle Crags is often very loose and dangerous. There are sections, however, that offer climbing much like that found in Pinnacles National Monument. As of this writing, no routes are known to have been led.

San Luis Obispo Bouldering

Bouldering on Bishop's Peak

Foothill Boulders

The trail from Foothill Blvd. to the Summit Blocks on Bishop's Peak passes through an oak tree grove before it reaches the rocky area. About 100 feet to the left of the trees lies a slanted crack (5.10a). There are also several difficult face problems on this same boulder.

Bouldering on Chlorissa.

Photo: Kevin Steele

Chlorissa and Pete
These are the most popular boulders in the San Luis Obispo area. If you are approaching the main climbing areas of Bishop's from Highland Drive you'll walk right by them. Chlorissa is the boulder on the right, Pete's Boulder is on the left. Both have excellent problems.

Boulder in the Woods
From Pete's Boulder walk left (south) across the hillside into the woods along a faint trail for several minutes. This boulder has longer problems (including a B1).

Hummingbird Boulder
This can be seen from the top of Chlorissa Boulder, uphill and left among the trees. Excellent overhanging advanced problems.

Potato Boulder
Sits several hundred feet below Shadow Wall in an oak grove. Cross the fence line above Chlorissa then cut right along a faint trail for 300 feet. The boulder is down the hillside in the trees. Potato Boulder has at least 10 or so top-rope routes 5.9 or harder. Twenty feet to the right of the tree is the Right-hand Potato route (5.11c) and the Left-hand Potato route up a seam.

The Mantel Boulders and the Far Boulder
Approach as for the Potato Boulder. Instead of dropping down the hillside, continue on for quite a ways to a cattle watering basin. Head up over the shoulder of the hillside, crossing a fence. The two low Mantel Boulders should be obvious. The Far Boulder can be seen 3/4 of the way down the hill, near a power pole.

San Luis Obispo Miscellanea

Cerro San Luis
There is a lot of rock in this area. A good boulder lies low on the hillside facing Highway 101.

Cal Poly Artificial Wall
Brain-child of Menzo Baird. Open only to Cal-Poly students.

Routes by Rating

Santa Barbara

Index

Bibliography

Dibblee Jr., Thomas W.; *Geology of the Central Santa Ynez Mountains*, 1966, California Division of Mines and Geology— Bulletin #186.

Dibblee Foundation, Thomas W. Jr.; *Geologic Maps*, Reference all quadrangles for Santa Barbara, Ventura, and San Luis Obispo counties.

Dickerson, Sharon Lewis; *Mountains of Fire*, 1990, EZ Nature Books.

Edwards, Steve; "Guide to Santa Barbara." *Rock and Ice Magazine #55*, May 1993

Ford Jr., Raymond; *Santa Barbara Day Hikes*, 1992, McNally and Loften Publishers.

Grant, Campbell; *The Rock Paintings of the Chumash*, 1965, University of California Press.

Gulyash, Peter; *Completely Off the Wall, A Climber's Guide to Bishop's Peak*, 1986; self-published.

Katz, David; *Getting High in L.A.*, 1990; self-published.

Klis, Ken; *Bishop's Peak and Environs / A Climber's Guide*, 1990; self-published.

Kroll, Dwight and Blench,James; *Happy Climbs of San Luis Obispo*, 1978; self-published.

News Press, Santa Barbara.

Skido, *Gold Coast Ice*, 1994, Skid Productions.

Sierra Club, Los Padres Chapter; *The Condor Call*.

Tucker, Stephen; "Climbing in the Santa Barbara Area." *Summit Magazine, Volume #21*, September 1975.

Tucker, Stephen; *Climbing in Santa Barbara and Ventura Counties*, 1981; self-published.

Voltz, Fred; *Ojai Hikes*, Self-published.

235

Colophon

This book is printed on 60 pound, sterling satin paper stock. The four-color cover is printed on Kivar 314 stock with a UV coated antique finish. The binding is Smythe Sewn. Type is set in Stone Serif and Stone Sans fonts, designed by Sumner Stone for Adobe.

Produced on Macintosh IIci, Macintosh IIsi, Macintosh Powerbook 160, Macintosh Classic, HP 1000LX, and Tristar 486/66 computers. Radius, Apple, Idek and Magnavox monitors were used. Photos and line art were scanned using the Logitech ScanMan hand-held grayscale scanner (for rough proofs) and the Hewlett-Packard ScanJetIIc (for high-resolution scans from which final output was imaged). Storage media included Quantum hard drives and the Bernoulli 150 removable drive. Laser proofs were made on RealTech Laser 960 and Hewlett Packard HP IV printers. Camera-ready copy was imaged on Scitex imagesetters.

Software included Microsoft Word 5.1, QuarkXpress 3.2, Deneba Canvas 3.5, Aldus Freehand 4.0, Aldus Photostyler, Digital Darkroom 2.1, Ofoto, and Panorama.

Printed on a Heidelberg 102z 28x40 sheet-fed press. Cover output on a Heidelberg model 102F.

Aerial Photography used for rock formation mapping was provided by Pacific Western Aerial Surveys of Santa Barbara using a Weiss 9x9 camera (152.70 focal length using Kodak Aerographic film) mounted in the belly of a twin engine Cessna flying at an altitude of 10,000 feet. Additional reconnaisance overflights were also made with Glen Bjorkman in his single-engine 1946 TaylorCraft and with Clint Harbers in his Robinson R-22 helicopter — both flying at sometimes questionable altitudes.

Bouldering and hiking breaks were taken at Rocky Hill, near Exeter, California.

Caffeine & Aebleskivers from Java Jungle and Valhalla. Tales and olde English ballads by JP. Musical accompaniment by Amos and Kevin on Fender, BlueRidge and Martin guitars.

Sonic Tendencies during design and layout sessions: Jimi Hendrix, The Cranberries, U2, The Orb, Eric Clapton, The Sex Pistols, Laurie Anderson, NIN, Eric Johnson, The Legendary Pink Dots, Belly, Pink Floyd, Robert Johnson, Bob Marley, Bonnie Raitt, Dead Can Dance, John Lee Hooker, Buddy Guy, Brian Eno and assorted ambient mixes.

Gratitudes: Linda and Annie and especially Christina for moral support and putting up with our kidnapping of Amos during numerous working visits. Welcome to the new world a new Steele who should pop forth about the same time this guide is finally printed.

Best Joke Heard: "It'll be finished in a month or two..."

Thanks to all of our good friends whom we've shared the mountains with.

KRISTY KLINE 4/ PARKING
@ FOOTHILL TRAILS 646-8602